HOW TO ENTER
SCREENPLAY CONTESTS...
AND WIN!
Second Edition

by Erik Joseph

LONE EAGLE PUBLISHING COMPANY, LLC™
1024 N. Orange Dr.
Hollywood, CA 90038
Phone 323.308.3400 or 800.815.0503
A division of IFILM® Corporation, www.ifilmpro.com

Printed in the United States of America

Cover design by Lindsay Albert
Creative direction by Sean Alatorre
Book design by Carla Green

Library of Congress Cataloging-in-Publication Data

Joseph, Erik.
    How to enter screenplay contests and win / Erik Joseph.--2nd ed.
      p. cm.
    Revised ed. of: How to enter screenplay contests & win! c1997.
    ISBN 1-58065-034-1
     1. Motion picture authorship. 2. Television authorship. 3. Contests--United States. I. Joseph, Erik. 1959- How to enter screenplay contests & win!
    II. Title.

    PN1996.J67   2001
    808.2'3--dc21   2001029472

Books may be purchased in bulk at special discounts for promotional or educational purposes. Special editions can be created to specifications. Inquiries for sales and distribution, textbook adoption, foreign language translation, editorial, and rights and permissions inquiries should be addressed to: Jeff Black, IFILM Publishing, 1024 N. Orange Dr., Hollywood, CA 90038 or send e-mail to: info@ifilm.com

Distributed to the trade by National Book Network, 800-462-6420

IFILM and Lone Eagle Publishing Company are registered trademarks.

For my wife Jenna

CONTENTS

> If a tree falls in the forest, and no one is around to hear it, does it make a sound?
>
> —Zen Koan

PREFACE

Screenwriting is a peculiar art. A completed screenplay is a tree falling in the forest with no one around.

First, the obvious: You'd better enjoy the solitary process of writing. Even the most successful, paid-in-advance screenwriters have screenplays languishing unproduced.

Next, how to get your screenplays read? Network and beg, until you get a decent agent to believe in you, then continue to network and beg (with a little more credibility), until a producer finally says, "Eureka, I have found it!"

And after all that, you're still not done. Next, "your" producer has to get a development executive to read it, who has to get his boss to read it, and, if they like it, they have to get a star actor and a name director to read it, which means their agents' assistants, then their agents, then—if all those people have liked it *and* the marketing department has chimed in with enthusiasm because it's high concept *and* the studio is willing to put an offer on the table—*then* the stars/directors will read it and you're in development.

But how to get the whole process started? A screenplay contest is a great beginning. Open to anyone, with or without credentials, relatives or contacts, screenplay contests assure you that *someone* will read your screenplay. Agents and executives often troll screenplay contests for finalists (not just the winners), and often actually request to read a screenplay. You can't get a better break than that.

So here are over one hundred screenplay contests just waiting to declare your screenplay the next hot thing. What are you waiting for?

INTRODUCTION TO
THE SECOND EDITION

When I wrote the first edition of this book in 1997, there were fewer than fifty viable screenwriting competitions. Today, there are over one hundred contests available. If we flashback to 1996, when I was developing the Nevada Screenwriters Competition for the Nevada Film Commission, there were only six screenwriting competitions to enter. Nevada still hosts the longest-running state sponsored screenwriting contest in the U.S. (I no longer live there nor run that contest. I've gone "Hollywood.")

Shortly after the first edition of this book was published, numerous new contest directors contacted me. They wanted to know, "How do we start and run a successful contest?" Well, it's good to see many of these contests running strong and included in this second edition. As a former contest director and judge, I applaud their successes. And as a former aspiring screenwriter, I cheer for the contest entrants.

Breaking in as a screenwriter can be an extraordinarily daunting task. We've all heard the scary statistics: "There are six million four-hundred thousand and two screenplays registered with the Writers Guild of America every day and only three are ever sold!"[1] And some of the Hollywood screenwriting books are so contrary. Each has its own take on structure, format, etc. (In the first edition I invented the Paradigmatic Super-Order. Did you see me winking?)

Here's all the advice in a nutshell: Buy the books, take the classes, find your island and write. Write one page, write thirty pages, write one hundred and forty pages. Then enter.

---

[1] In fact, 40,000 pieces of material were registered with the Writers Guild in 2000, and fewer than 500 films were produced and distributed.

In 1997, I calculated over three million dollars in guaranteed cash available to writers via screenwriting contests, plus other outstanding prizes and opportunities. What's it worth today? Over ten times as much! You can even get your short script made and distributed. Talk about a career kickstart.

So, how can anyone with the desire to tell a story on paper get involved in the screenwriting contest boon? Write it right and write it well. I'm going to let the experts (authors, teachers, writers, judges, winners, contest directors) tell you how to do that. Look for the "Expert Tip" sidebars throughout this edition. How do you beat a contest's odds? Look for the "Best Advice" offered by the contest directors themselves. Here's My Best Advice: write less, say more.

Which contests should you enter? That's up to you. Got a minute? Try the Page One Screenwriting Contest. What's your specialty: Westerns? Female protagonist? African-American? Arizona? Sci-Fi? Sitcoms?

Which contests are most respected in the industry? Too lofty a question for me, so I asked a Hollywood-based Zen Master/screenwriter/producer/kickboxing instructor and this was his answer: a good script.

I said it then and I'll say it now: winning a screenplay contest is the best and most affordable way to get your screenplay noticed, optioned, sold and produced. Guaranteed prizes, certified promises, beatable odds. Minimal investment for maximum return.

Now it's time to stop reading the books, skip the class and actually write. Sound contrary to the advice given earlier? How typically Hollywood of me.

—*Erik Joseph*

WHICH TO ENTER?

You can't enter all of them. And I wouldn't suggest picking one or two out and writing a script just for them, either, unless you have an idea burning in your head that just happens to match their requirements. More convenient is to keep writing what *you* want to write, then search for a contest for which your favorite screenplay is appropriate. Look at the "purpose," the "rules" and the "categories" for suitability. There's no point in sending your urban horror story to a Southwestern state contest that wants a local romance to help publicize its great outdoors. The genre index in the back of this book should help you with that.

Let's face it, there are probably a few scams out there; maybe even a lot of them. Avoid like the plague any contest that says "All entries become the property of the sponsor." Intellectual property should never be assigned without agency consultation, and never without good financial compensation.

Compare their entry fees. $35 to $45 seems to be about standard. Check out their website to see just how professional they are. Check their prizes. Money is always good. Trips to festivals are fun and give you the opportunity to network with industry types.

Who's behind them? Film festivals and state film commissions are probably pretty earnest, as are large institutions, such as the Academy of Motion Pictures Arts and Sciences, or a reputable studio or a network. Production companies are always on the lookout for good scripts, but if they really have financing, they're probably inundated with top agent submissions already. Still, the new digital filmmaking is coming on strong. Any way to get your film made and seen is great.

A WORD ON AGENTS

Just getting a good agent out of a contest would be terrific. You absolutely need one in Hollywood. If the agency is not signatory to the Writers' Guild of America, however, forget them. Unless you are a "name," you'll need an agent in Hollywood or New York. Out of sight, out of mind. If you're not there yourself, your agent needs to be.

Go with the agent, not the agency. He or she is the one you're counting on to get your screenplay read. Most large agencies use a "committee" method now — someone covering each network and studio, watching for upcoming assignments, etc. — but make sure you have someone specific you value who will return your calls. Large agencies have power in packaging, which is pervasive today (if you want Tom Cruise or Bruce Willis to read your script, you had better be with his agency), but small agencies are probably better for writers starting out. You're less likely to get lost, and the agent will probably work harder to jump start your career.

SUPPOSE YOU WIN?!

Cooperate as much as possible with the contest's publicity machine. Let them exploit you to the local, regional and national media. Your name and photo may pop up in your hometown newspaper. You may shake the hand of a Governor. Your name likely will appear in reference books, on Internet sites and in festival programs. You may be interviewed for *How To Enter Screenplay Contests & Win! 3rd Edition.* What's all this worth? Publicity.

A few contests guarantee to produce all or a portion of your script. Other contests option your script for "possible production." Make sure you have an experienced entertainment lawyer or agent represent you if they offer an option or sale.

THE RULES

My research suggests that roughly 25 percent of all submissions are automatically eliminated due to unprofessional format, other eligibility or stylistic misjudgments or simply not following the rules. Just before you proof your screenplay for the last time, look closely at the contest rules and requirements.

FINALLY, KEEP IN MIND...

Deadlines dates are "postmarked by," and contest information changes from year to year, so always contact the contest before submitting. Information provided here is to the best of the author's efforts.

THE CONTESTS

ALL SHE WROTE SCREENPLAY CONTEST

Purpose:	To promote the presence of women in the industry.
Entry fee:	$25 early, $40 standard
Year began:	1998
Categories:	All
Sponsor:	Final Draft and others
Address:	P.O. Box 1262 Grass Valley, CA 95945
Fax:	(530) 272-6688
Email:	info@allshewrote.com
Website:	www.allshewrote.com
Deadline:	April 7 annually
Rules:	Open to all female writers who do not earn a living as screenwriters or who are not considered "professional" screenwriters. Entered screenplays must not have been previously optioned, sold or produced. Please see website for more.
Best Advice:	Follow the regulations and do not add ephemera to your submission (such as resumes, etc.).
Director:	Indigo Dawson
Judges:	It varies each year; Hollywood executives and producers.
Cash prizes:	$1,000 and up.
Non-cash prizes:	Final Draft Software and much more; see website.

ALLIANCE SCREENPLAY COMPETITION

Purpose:	To nurture, support and develop relationships with new and innovative screenwriting talent. We are looking for individuals with unique voices, imaginative ideas and unconventional storytelling approaches.
Entry fee:	Early: $35, Final: $45
Year began:	1999
Categories:	Feature length film
Sponsor:	Alliance Entertainment
Address:	Alliance Screenplay Competition Alliance Entertainment 3101 Howell Mill Rd. #125 Atlanta, GA 30327
Fax:	(404) 355-3487
Email:	allianceent@aol.com
Website:	www.allianceentertainment.com (rules, application, purpose, deadlines, awards)
Deadline:	Early: May 15, Final: June 15
Rules:	90-130 pages, standard industry format, bound with brads. Must be the original work of author; no adaptations accepted. Multiple submissions accepted. Do not put your name on the cover or any other page of the script. Screenplays will not be returned without SASE.
Best Advice:	An interesting, intellectual and well-written plot; a unique and distinguished story; strong characters; unexpected twist; great climax/resolution; try to be alternative instead of mainstream.
Director:	Patson Ohm, Coordinator
Judges:	Educators and professional screenwriters
Cash prizes:	$1,000.
Non-cash prizes:	Possible option/production deals.
Success story:	1999 winner is working in Asia with a television production company.

AMERICAN ACCOLADES
SCREENWRITING COMPETITION

Purpose:	To provide an outlet for emerging talent and undiscovered screenplays.
Entry fee:	$45
Year began:	1999
Categories:	Drama, Thriller/Horror, Comedy, Sci-Fi, Action/Adventure, Other
Sponsor:	The American Accolades
Address:	The American Accolades Screenwriting Competition 2118 Wilshire Blvd. #160B Santa Monica, CA 90403
Fax:	(310) 453-2523
Email:	info@americanaccolades.com
Website:	www.americanaccolades.com (Rules/regulations, application form, synopsis form, Q & A [do's and don'ts], accolades, hall of fame, more)
Deadline:	December 31
Rules:	Include application/release form, entry fee, synopsis, two copies of the script. Title page should include author name, phone number, email. No other page should have identifying information on it. Standard industry format, 3-hole punched, bound. No longer than 135 pages. Write name of screenplay on bound edge. Entries will not be returned. Register the script for your own protection. Work cannot have been optioned, produced or sold prior to time of submission. Must be original work of author. If based on another source, writer must provide a clearance statement in writing.
Director:	Peter Scott (see following interview)

Judges: Industry professionals which may include any of the
                     following: film school professors, free-lance readers,
                     executives and/or producers. Feedback provided.
                     Comments include where the writer placed com-
                     pared to other scripts (e.g., top 10 percent, 20 per-
                     cent, 50 percent, etc.) and what qualities the
                     judges most liked and disliked about the script.

Cash Prizes: Grand prize: $2,500; genre $500.

Non-cash prizes: Comprehensive screenplay analysis, entry into the
                     Accolades Hall of Fame, posted on website.

> **"**The first ten pages of a feature script are
> the most important.**"**
>
> —from *How To Sell Your Screenplay:*
> *The Real Rules of Film and*
> *Television Screenwriting*
> by Carl Sautter
>
> (Especially if you consider that the
> reader might put it down after that if
> they're not sufficiently intrigued.)

AMERICAN ACCOLADES TV

Purpose:	To provide an outlet for emerging writing talent.
Entry fee:	1/2 hour $35, 1 hour $45, MOW $50
Year began:	2000
Categories:	1/2 hour (any show), 1/2 hour pilot (original show), 1 hour (any show), 1 hour pilot MOW (original show)
Sponsor:	American Accolades
Address:	Accolades TV 2118 Wilshire Blvd. #160B Santa Monica, CA 90403
Fax:	(310) 453-2523
Email:	info@americanaccolades.com
Website:	www.americanaccolades.com/accoladestv.htm
Deadline:	July 31
Rules:	Application/Release forms, synopsis, two copies of script. See website for more instructions on formatting and style elements.
Best Advice:	Don't cheat your margins. See website Q & A for more.
Director:	Peter Scott (see following interview)
Cash Prizes:	Grand prize: $700; genre: $300.
Non-cash prizes:	Twelve finalists enter Accolade TV Hall of Fame, website publicity, exposure to industry professionals.

INTERVIEW

INTERVIEW

with Peter Scott, Contest Director, American Accolades

What is your background with American Accolades?
The 2000 American Accolades is my third year as contest director. As Director, I assemble the teams of judges, oversee the story meetings and judging process, and ensure that the competition takes place on a level playing field. American Accolades offers an annual television and full-length screenplay competition.

How did you start in the entertainment industry?
I worked for ten years in television and film, including sales, production and studio work. I worked for Bungalow Productions, then ICM, where I was an agent trainee with Tom Strickler. I worked in the television literary division. One of our clients was Randy McCormick (former Nicholl Fellowship winner). (More can be read about Peter Scott's industry background in Thom Taylor's book *The Big Deal: Hollywood's Million Dollar Spec Script Market.*)

How have you helped make the American Accolades contests stand out from other writing competitions?
American Accolades contests offer the total package: Hollywood judges, cash prizes, low entry fee, multiple genre categories, feedback to all writers. In addition, finalists receive professional studio-style coverage from the Academy Writers Clinic (AcademyWriters.com), publicity and meetings with high-profile industry executives. Our mission has always been to find and usher emerging writing talent into the mainstream marketplace.

Why do you feel screenwriting contests have become so popular in the last few years?
Screenwriting contests offer a unique channel for writers to access an industry that remains relatively closed to newcomers. Designed properly, contests offer cash prizes, access, and feedback for writers. It's no secret that a screenplay often gets one chance in a million when sent out as a spec. For this reason, writers often enter contests to gauge their progress. From the perspective of Hollywood-ites, contests offer a filtration process and a systematic way to sort through the multitude of screenplays that producers, executives

and agents all have an interest in discovering, but may not have the time to read. Winning a mainstream contest is the equivalent of a professional referral.

The recent explosion of new contests revolves around the advent and popularity of the Internet. Many new competitions on the web offer important opportunities for writers. On the other hand, protect yourself—research the contest and contest director's credentials.

What's your best advice to winners of a contest?
Buckle up! Winners of major competitions are approached by numerous executives and representatives—resulting in a writer's need to stay balanced. The first step should involve securing the best representation possible (agent, manager and/or entertainment attorney, or all three). When a barrage of phone calls and emails hit the winning writer's desk, the writer should keep his or her excitement in check and explain that they are planning to take meetings with representatives within a specific window of time. Next come meetings with producers and studio executives.

Even if the claim is exaggerated, this will create a desirable "supply and demand" scenario when the writer attempts to sell their work to representatives. When agents ask you about others you are meeting, use the stock phrase "I don't want to jinx anything," which is Hollywood code for "none of your business." Finally, telling agents that you are following up your agency meetings with production company meetings may make them wish to sign you before you strike gold.

When you speak to agents, be prepared to send them your material—a bio and other screenplays or treatments that you have written. Send your best work, rather than a multitude of unpolished material. The process of agents evaluating you and your material usually takes a while.

In the meantime, send a query letter to production companies. Highlight your contest win and pitch your work. If a company likes your material, a production executive may help you secure an agent.

AMERICAN CINEMA FOUNDATION
SCREENWRITING COMPETITION

Purpose:
To elicit scripts which are suitable for either theatrical or television production and which tell a positive story about specific fundamental values and their importance to society.

Entry fee:
$30

Year began:
1995

Categories:
Any writer, anywhere. Check with contest for current theme. Scripts must be suitable for theatrical or television production.

Sponsor:
The Board of Trustees of the American Cinema Foundation

Address:
Screenwriting Competition
American Cinema Foundation
9911 W. Pico Blvd. #510
Los Angeles, CA 90035

Phone:
(310) 286-9420

Fax:
(310) 286-7914

Email:
acinema@cinemafoundation.com

Website:
www.cinemafoundation.com
(Regulations, theme, submitting, deadlines, judging criteria, prizes, announcements)

Deadline:
May 31

Rules:
This is a themed competition. Visit our website for complete rules and guidelines.

Best Advice:
Adhere to the theme.

Director:
Gary McVey

Judges:
Professionals working in the entertainment industry (agents, writers, producers, directors and production personnel).

Cash prizes:
First place: $10,000; second place: $5,000; third place: $5,000.

Success stories:
So far, two winning scripts have been optioned.

AMERICAN DREAM FACTORY

Purpose:	To find the perfect screenplay to pitch to a Hollywood executive.
Entry fee:	$50 (U.S.)
Year began:	2001
Categories:	All genres accepted.
Address:	Shoppers World Postal Outlet 3003 Danforth Ave. PO Box 93657 Toronto, Canada, M4C 5R5
Email:	info@americandreamfactory.com
Website:	www.americandreamfactory.com
Deadline:	July 1
Rules:	See website.
Best Advice:	It takes lights, camera and action to get a movie going.
Cash prizes:	$3,500 (U.S.)
Non-cash prizes:	Runner-ups will also be pitched to executives.

> **"**Put a time limit on the action your character takes and you'll have more suspense in your story.**"**
>
> —from *Blueprint For Writing: a Writer's Guide To Creativity, Craft and Career* by Rachel Friedman Ballon, Ph.D.

AMERICAN DREAMER

Purpose:	To encourage new, groundbreaking writers to pursue careers in the fine art of screenwriting.
Entry fee:	Early: $50, Final: $60
Year began:	1998
Categories:	Full-length feature screenplays, unfinished screenplays (first ten pages)
Sponsor:	American Dreamer Independent Filmworks Inc.
Address:	American Dreamer independent Filmworks Inc. P.O. Box 20457 Seattle, WA 98102
Phone:	(206) 325-0451
Fax:	(206) 320-7724
Email:	comments@adfilmworks.com
Website:	www.adfilmworks.com (Application, rules, studio-ready tip sheet, results, FAQ's, references, more)
Deadline:	Early: July 4, Final: August 5
Rules:	Original work, in English. (See website for complete rules and application procedures.)
Best Advice:	Scripts are evaluated on various levels, including but not limited to, ability to create a visual narrative, writing style and total production potential.
Judges:	Varies. Contest director makes final decision.
Cash prizes:	$5,000 (acquisition fee; if no script is acquired, contest will refund all entry fees).
Non-cash prizes:	Script feedback, publicity.

AMERICAN SCREENWRITERS ASSOCIATION AND WRITER'S DIGEST INTERNATIONAL SCREENPLAY COMPETITION

Purpose:	To assist and recognize screenwriters through networking and education.
Entry fee:	$40 for ASA members, $50 for non-members
Year began:	2001
Categories:	All genres accepted.
Sponsor:	American Screenwriters Association and Writer's Digest
Address:	F & W Publications 1507 Dana Avenue Cincinnati, OH 45207
Phone:	(513) 731-9212
Email:	competitions@fwpubs.com
Website:	www.writersdigest.com or www.asascriptwriters.com
Deadline:	October 31, 2001
Rules:	See guidelines on the website.
Cash prizes:	More than $10,000 in cash and prizes. Please see website for details.
Non-cash prizes:	See website.

THE AMERICAN SCREENWRITERS ASSOCIATION'S COMMON SUBMISSION PROBLEMS TO AVOID

There are ASA Chapters and Affiliate Member Groups in Chicago, Cincinnati, Dayton, Twin Falls, Washington D.C., Maryland, Maine and Virginia. Check out the ASA website at www.asascreenwriter.com

1. Prepare your script according to competition guidelines. Read competition guidelines thoroughly, then read them again. When you think you are ready to submit your script, read them one last time. Most competitions will immediately disqualify you and most entry fees are nonrefundable. This is a professional business so you *must* learn proper script formatting and submission. On the other hand, don't read between the lines of the competition. Sometimes people fret over every little detail and read into the rules things that aren't there.

2. Match your synopsis with your script. Sometimes writers make changes to their script after developing a synopsis and forget to update the synopsis. Other times the synopsis is used to "pump up" the script. If your synopsis doesn't match your script you will lose the reader and thus kill interest in your script.

3. Avoid one-dimensional characters. A defining point of whether a judge will advance your script centers on three-dimensional characters. Characters should leap off the page. Are your characters lifeless or bland? Here's a good test. Get some friends together and do a reading of the script. Listen carefully. You will hear the problem areas and character weaknesses. If you don't, your friends will!

4. Avoid thin plots. We've all heard the cliché about there not being any more original ideas because Shakespeare introduced them all. Whether you believe that or not, the point is to find a new twist to an idea. There have been a hundred romantic movies but there are big differences between *Casablanca, Sleepless in Seattle* and *Never Been Kissed*. Be original and find a new way to get us to pay to see your movie.

5. Do your homework. If you haven't read books on screenwriting, taken a screenwriting seminar on format and structure, or studied information in screenwriting publications, you are not ready to enter!

AMERICA'S BEST HIGH SCHOOL
WRITING COMPETITION

Purpose:	To support education by supporting high school level screenwriters.
Entry fee:	$3
Year began:	1996
Categories:	Screenplays or television scripts (original or existing shows); class projects are also accepted.
Sponsor:	The Writer's Foundation
Address:	The Writer's Foundation 3936 S. Semoran Blvd. #368 Orlando, FL 32822
Phone:	(407) 894-9001
Fax:	(407) 894-5547
Deadline:	March 1
Rules:	High School students only. Screenplays: Submit the first ten pages and a synopsis of not more than two double-spaced pages. TV scripts: submit a cast description and synopsis. Write for more rules.
Best Advice:	Use professional format. Ask yourself: Will Hollywood make this movie? Don't be afraid of criticism because you can always get better as a writer.
Director:	Bob Cope
Judges:	The Writer's Foundation
Non-cash prizes:	Prizes and publicity.

AMERICA'S BEST WRITING COMPETITION

Purpose:	To focus attention on the importance of writers in our society and the immense contributions they make to our worldwide community.
Entry fee:	TV Sitcom: $25, TV Drama: $25, Screenplay: $35 (These are suggested donations; America's Best Writing Competition is a not-for-profit organization.)
Year began:	1990
Categories:	Screenplay, Television Drama, Television Sitcom
Sponsor:	The Writer's Foundation
Address:	The Writer's Foundation 3936 S. Semoran Blvd. #368 Orlando, FL 32822
Phone:	(407) 894-9001
Fax:	(407) 894-5547
Deadline:	March 6
Rules:	Write for Rules.
Best Advice:	Get to the point—tone, story—in the first ten pages or the judges won't continue to read. Show off from the very first page. If you can't write a logline, you may want to think about writing a novel. Readers want to read something that will sell. Use professional format.
Director:	Bob Cope
Judges:	The Writer's Foundation
Cash prizes:	Screenplay: $10,00; TV Drama: $1,000; TV Sitcom: $1,000.
Non-cash prizes:	Publicity.

ARGYLE GLOBAL SCRIPT SEARCH

Purpose:	To discover, reward and promote new screenwriting talent.
Entry fee:	Early: $39.50, Standard: $44.50, Final: $49.50
Categories:	Open to all writers 18 and older, all genres accepted.
Sponsor:	Argyle Productions
Address:	Argyle Global Script Search Argyle Productions 2054 N. Argyle Ave. #116 Hollywood, CA 90068
Fax:	(323) 871-2909
Email:	ArgylePr@aol.com
Deadline:	Early: March 1, Standard: May 1, Final: June 5
Rules:	Written in English, industry format, bound with brads. Writers of produced scripts or who have sold a script for more than $10,000 are not eligible. No adaptations. Multiple submissions accepted. Contact information should only appear on application form and cover. Include an index card with contact information. Send SASE for confirmation.
Director:	Christopher Schultz, Coordinator
Judges:	Argyle Productions
Cash prizes:	Up to $3,500.
Non-cash prizes:	Publicity, literary agent contacts, preparation of budget, marketing plan, line-by-line critique.

AUSTIN HEART OF FILM
SCREENPLAY COMPETITION

Purpose:	To acknowledge the achievements of new screenwriters.
Entry fee:	$40
Year began:	1996
Categories:	Adult/Mature, Children/Family, Comedy
Sponsor:	Austin Film Festival
Address:	Austin Heart of Film Screenplay Competition 1604 Nueces Austin, TX 78701-1106
Phone:	(800) 310-FEST and (512) 478-4795
Fax:	(512) 478-6205
Email:	austinfilm@aol.com
Website:	www.austinfilmfestival.com (Entry form, previous winners, more)
Deadline:	May 15
Rules:	Open to writers who do not earn a living writing for television or film. Property must not have been optioned or sold prior to entering, and must be original work of author (or author must submit a clearance statement). Semi-finalists and beyond from previous competitions are not eligible. Multiple submissions are acceptable. We suggest you register your script. Send proper submission materials. Industry standard format, 90-130 pages (single or double-sided), three-hole punched and bound with brads. Only the title should appear on the front card stock cover. A second title page should be included with title, author's name, address and phone number. Author's name must not appear anywhere else in the script. Must also include a two-sentence synopsis. Screenplays will not be returned. Include SASE for acknowledgement.
Best Advice:	Follow industry format, follow the guidelines and present your best work.

Director:	B.J. Burrow
Judges:	Panel of industry development executives and producers.
Cash prizes:	Adult and family catagory, first place: $4,000; comedy catagory, first place: $1,000.
Non-cash prizes:	Round trip airfare (up to $500), up to four nights accommodation (up to $500), complimentary All-Access Producer's Pass to the Film Festival and Screenwriters Conference, award.
Success story:	Options, some writers produced.

> **"**Enable a sympathetic character to overcome a series of increasingly difficult, seemingly insurmountable obstacles and achieve a compelling desire. That, in about two dozen words, is what almost every successful feature film has ever done. **"**
>
> —from *Writing Screenplays That Sell*
> by Michael Hauge

TIPS

from *Secrets Of Screenplay Structure* by Linda J. Cowgill

CAUSE AND EFFECT
There should be nothing which is not clearly caused by what precedes, and nothing which is not clearly the cause of what follows.

THEME
The theme is illustrated on the plotting of the film's action and is not relegated to speeches characters make; it is dramatized and acted out in the interrelationships between the characters.

PLOT
Structuring the plot of a great film is distilling from all the elements of screenwriting—concept, characterization, theme, story, action, obstacles—a sequence of scenes that builds suspense, utilizes surprise and logically makes sense of all the factors while saying something meaningful by the end.

SHOW, DON'T TELL
Scenes are strongest when they do not depend upon dialogue to communicate their entire meaning.

GREAT DIALOGUE
Great dialogue should be clear and understandable the first time you hear it, yet also create the illusion of real conversation.

CLUMSY DIALOGUE
When names are used in every other line of dialogue, it sounds clumsy and unnatural. When a writer overuses character names in dialogue, it is usually an indication that he does not know his creations as well as he should.

BAD KITTY FILMS SCREENPLAY COMPETITION

Purpose:	To discover new, fresh stories, and to assist writers by offering coverage and industry contacts.
Entry fee:	$45
Year began:	1998
Categories:	Feature, Short Subject
Sponsor:	Bad Kitty Films
Address:	Bad Kitty Films Screenplay Competition 2431 Mission Street San Francisco, CA 94110
Phone:	(408) 642-MEOW
Fax:	(415) 723-7378
Email:	info@badkittyfilms.com
Website:	www.badkittyfilms.com (Guidelines, entry form, more.)
Deadline:	August 31
Rules:	Non-documentary scripts. Feature should be 80-125 pages, short subject 15-30 pages. Industry format, 2-3 hole punched and fastened with brads, card stock cover. Title *only* on the card stock cover. Do not put author's name on the title sheet. Multiple submissions acceptable. We strongly suggest you register your script. Must be sole property of author, and must not have been sold or optioned at time of submission. Not adhering to the guidelines may result in disqualification. Be careful!
Best Advice:	There is no formula. Good, character-driven pieces that explore rich themes are what speak to our judges. Hone your work, get feedback from as many people as you can, know your characters and make sure they feel real to you. Ask yourself: Is this a story I would pay money to see?
Director:	Sandra Hall, Administrator

Judges: Established screenwriters, award-winning producers and directors, film school graduates and respected agency representatives.

Cash prizes: Feature $300, Short Subject $100.

Non-cash prizes: Award of Achievement, script coverage, option and development consideration, introduction to top writing agents.

Success story: Many scripts optioned (not just winning scripts), other writers signed with agencies.

" If you include more than six parenthetical directions within your entire screenplay, you've got too many . **"**

—from *Writing Screenplays That Sell*
by Michael Hauge

" No parentheticals in dialogue. Let the director or actor decide how to say the lines. **"**

—from *Blueprint For Writing: a Writer's Guide To Creativity, Craft and Career*
by Rachel Friedman Ballon, Ph.D.

" Do not direct actors how to say the lines or how to move. **"**

—from *Screenwriting Tricks of the Trade*
by William Froug

BARE BONES INTERNATIONAL SCREENPLAY COMPETITION

Purpose:	To find quality screenplays for Bare Bones projects that can be produced for less than one million dollars.
Entry fee:	Early: $35, Final: $45
Year began:	1999
Categories:	All genres; budgeted at less than $1,000,000
Sponsor:	Bare Bones International Film Festival
Address:	Bare Bones Screenplay Competition 401 W. Broadway, 2nd Fl. P.O. Box 2017 Muskogee, OK 74402
Phone:	(918) 483-9701
Email:	barebonesmoviemakers@juno.com
Website:	www.barebonesfilmfestival.bizland.com
Deadline:	Early: before December 30, Final: after December 30
Rules:	Original work, maximum 120 pages, standard industry format, numbered pages, may be two-sided, 3-hole punched, bound with card stock covers, fastened with brads. Only the title should appear on the first page. The second page should have the title, author, address, phone number. Do not put author's name anywhere else on the script. We suggest WGA registration.
Best Advice:	Write a compelling story that makes the reader not want to stop reading until they reach the end.
Director:	Shiron Butterfly Ray
Judges:	Bare Bones production staff
Cash prizes:	Check website.
Non-cash prizes:	Products, services, travel, awards luncheon, readings.

BEST IN THE WEST
SCREENWRITING COMPETITION

Purpose:	To promote and expose the beauty and uniqueness of the West to the rest of the world, and to encourage quality films. Will mentor fledgling writers, refine their skills, encourage their creativity. (Best in the West Screenwriting Competition is a nonprofit organization.)
Entry fee:	$35
Year began:	1998
Categories:	Old West—any story taking place west of the Mississippi River prior to 1930; New West—any story taking place west of the Mississippi River after 1931.
Sponsor:	Best in the West
Address:	Best in the West Screenwriting Competition 299 Eastview Dr. Durango, CO 81301
Phone:	(970) 382-9530
Fax:	(970) 382-9529
Email:	westscript@rmi.net
Website:	www.home.rmi.net/~westscript/index.html. (Purpose, rules, application/release, requirements, winners, judges.)
Deadline:	July 1
Rules:	No longer than 125 pages, industry format, not optioned prior to submission. Must include one page synopsis, logline, application, release form and entry fee.
Best Advice:	Go through your screenplay and ask yourself on each scene, "Have I seen this before?" If the answer is yes then ask yourself, "How can I make it unique?" Check your spelling and grammar. Be careful not to overwrite. Write an opening that grabs the reader.
Director:	Shannon Richardson

Judges: One winner, one runner-up and three other finalists in each category. First round is judged by the Inkslingers—a professional writing organization. Final round judged by industry professionals in Hollywood.

Non-cash prizes: Trophies presented during the Western Film Festival, exposure to industry professionals, publicity, coverage/comments.

Success story: Some optioned, some gained management.

❝ Write what you know. It is always better to write about some personal experience about which you feel passionate.**❞**

—from *Blueprint For Writing: a Writer's Guide To Creativity, Craft and Career* by Rachel Friedman Ballon, Ph.D.

(Well, sometimes. Shakespeare never visited Venice. It's unlikely Tolkien ever saw Middle Earth. There are surely ten times as many police procedurals than there are ex-policemen writing mysteries. The rest just did good research. Let's simplify: do your homework.)

BIG AUSTRALIAN INTERNATIONAL SCREENWRITING COMPETITION

Purpose: To connect writers with professionals in Australia and worldwide.

Entry fee: Early: $65, Standard: $75, Final: $85

Year began: 1999

Categories: Any genre feature film screenplay.

Sponsor: The Source Worldwide Scriptservice

Address: Big Australian International Screenwriting Competition Head Office
94 Hargrave St.
Paddington, Sydney NS 2025

Phone: 61 (7) 5538-4970 or 61 (2) 9326 1344

Fax: 61 (7) 5538-4465 or 61 (2) 9326 1283

Email: info@thesource.com.au

Website: www.thesource.com.au
(Prizes, rules, results, judges, questions, forms, script format, tips, dates, fees, registration, sponsors, release, entries.)

Deadline: September 30

Rules: See website.

Best Advice: Be original. Act professional—make every word count. (See website "Screenwriting Tips.")

Director: Allan Hawley Jacobs

Judges: Professionals in the industry—agents, producers, managers.

Cash prizes: Grand prize: $10,000; ten finalists: $1,000.

Non-cash prizes: Grand prize winner also receives a two-week trip for two to the destination of their choice: Hollywood, Sydney, Hawaii, Gold Coast. The grand prize winner and ten finalists also are offered representation and will be submitted to industry professionals; twenty semi-finalists receive in-depth script analysis.

Success story: Bruce Beresford is to direct a semi-finalist; others optioned.

BLUE SKY INTERNATIONAL FILM FESTIVAL'S SCREENPLAY COMPETITION

Purpose:	Dedicated to the discovery of new writing talent.
Entry fee:	$25
Year began:	1998
Categories:	Feature length, any genre. Open to anyone.
Sponsor:	Blue Sky International Film Festival
Address:	Blue Sky International Film Festival 4185 Paradise Rd. #2009 Las Vegas, NV 89109
Phone:	(702) 737-3313
Email:	bsiff98@aol.com
Website:	www.bsiff.com (Applications, awards, sponsors, Las Vegas weather, rooms and rates, logo store.)
Deadline:	July 14
Rules:	Feature length, no television episodes.
Best Advice:	Follow the guidelines for submitting to the last letter and only submit a polished, final draft. Don't expect the competition to be your writing school. Do expect producers to be watching and eager to find their next project.
Director:	Jeffrey Matthews Hill, Executive Producer
Judges:	Industry professionals—producers, writers.
Cash prizes:	$1,000.
Non-cash prizes:	Winning script is performed "live" by the Blue Sky Players.
Success story:	Options, acquired agents or managers.

BLUECAT SCREENPLAY COMPETITION

Purpose: To expose the great undiscovered screenplays, which exist, and to become a virtual lightning rod for these works. We want to find scripts that absolutely should be produced into films. We want to help change the lives of the writers we recognize.

Entry fee: $20 per two screenplays

Year began: 1998

Categories: All genres accepted.

Sponsor: BlueCat Productions

Address: The BlueCat Screenplay Competition
P.O. Box 2630
Hollywood, CA 90028

Email: info@bluecatscreenplay.com

Website: www.bluecatscreenplay.com
(Submission information, prizes, announcements, FAQ, rules and guidelines, common missteps.)

Deadline: February 1

Rules: Original, unsold works. Must be sole property of author. Do not put name/address on cover and do not send with a literary agency cover. The cover should only include the title. Scripts will not be returned. Do not send originals. No substitutions or corrected drafts or pages will be accepted. Screenplays must be in English and standard industry format. Minimum 80 pages in length, no maximum. Three-hole punched, bound with brads.

Best Advice: See website for Common Missteps.

Director: Gordon Hoffman, Founder

Judges: BlueCat staff and WGA members

Cash prizes: $3,000.

Non-cash prizes: Twenty finalists honored in trade publications, personal phone call with feedback.

BRECKENRIDGE FESTIVAL OF FILM
SCREENPLAY COMPETITION

Purpose:	To foster a relaxed atmosphere where writers are accessible to professionals and professionals are accessible to writers.
Entry fee:	Early: $35, Final: $40
Year began:	Films: 1980; Screenplays: 1997
Categories:	Adult Drama, Children/Family, Comedy, Action/Adventure
Sponsor:	Breckenridge Festival of Film
Address:	Breckenridge Festival of Film P.O. Box 718 Breckenridge, CO 80424
Phone:	(970) 453-2692
Fax:	(970) 453-2692
Email:	filmfest@brecknet.com
Website:	www.brecknet.com/bff/home.html
Deadline:	Early: April 28, Final: after April 28 until May 31
Rules:	Standard industry format, between 90-130 pages. Must be original works and must not have been optioned or sold at time of submission. Include a short synopsis.
Best Advice:	Write well and use screenwriting software. Check spelling and grammar.
Director:	Shawnna Gauss
Judges:	A committee of reviewers from the community, and an executive panel of writers, producers and film distributors.
Non-cash prizes:	Free lodging and airport transportation are provided for invited filmmakers and screenwriters during the event.

BROOKS PHARMACY SCREENPLAY COMPETITION, PART OF THE RHODE ISLAND INTERNATIONAL FILM FESTIVAL

Purpose: To honor creativity, innovation, vision, originality and the use of language. The key element is that of communication and how it complements and is transformed by the language of film.

Entry fee: $30

Year began: 2000

Categories: The Festival accepts screenplays in all genres. The Rhode Island International Film Festival is one of only three broadly focused, independent festivals in New England accepting works of any type (dramatic, documentary, experimental), on any subject matter and in any genre.

Sponsor: Brooks Pharmacy, Final Draft, *Scr(i)pt* magazine,

Address: Brooks Pharmacy Screenplay Competition
c/o Rhode Island International Film Festival
P.O. Box 162
Newport, RI 02840

Phone: (401) 861-4445

Fax: (401) 847-7590

Email: flicksart@aol.com

Website: www.film-festival.org and www.rifilmfest.org (Rules, application, more.)

Deadline: Early Deadline: April 1
Late Deadline: May 15
(Note: These are annual deadlines and do not change from year to year.)

Rules:	Screenplays cannot have been sold or optioned prior to or at the time of submission. Screenplays must be standard feature film length (90-130 pages) and standard U.S. format only. Screenplays may not have been produced or won completion awards at other festivals. Screenplays must be copyrighted or WGA registered and must be the original work of the applicant. Screenplays must be in English. Screenplays must be completed by entry deadline and have been written after 1998. The competition is open to all writers of feature length screenplays. Applicant must be over the age of 18 years.
Entry Procedure:	Only the title should appear on the cover page of the screenplay. The applicant's name should not appear on the cover or any other page of the screenplay. Judges will not be aware of the entrant's name. Entry must include an application and payment. Keep a copy of your completed application form for reference. For confirmation that we have received your entry, include a self-addressed stamped postcard. There is no limit to the number of entries per entrant provided separate applications and submission fees accompany each entry. The Festival is not responsible for screenplays lost or damaged in transit. Screenplays will not be returned. Please make a copy of your screenplay for your files.
Best Advice:	Apply early. Most entries arrive just before our deadline and it creates a crunch for our judges. Because each title is reviewed by three different judges, early applicants have an advantage with greater time being spent on their work.
Director:	George T. Marshall, Executive Director; Elizabeth N. Galligan, Managing Director; Eleyne Austen Sharp, Screenplay Competition Director
Judges:	Screenplays are judged by a jury of distinguished panel of industry professionals, peers and film fans. Consultants to the competition and to the ScriptBiz program include Skip Press, Author, *Writer's Guide to Hollywood Producers, Directors, and Screenwriter's Agents* and Richard William Krevolin, Professor, USC Film School, *Screenwriting from the Soul.*

Cash prizes: The grand prize winner will receive cash and prizes valued at $2,000, including Final Draft software. The grand prize winner will have segments of the work produced during the Festival's Master Class on Production: "Take One, Two, Three: Filmmaking with the Pros," which features the participation of a noted director each year. In the past, directors have included Robert Downey Sr., Lloyd Kaufman and Richard Schenkman.

Non-cash prizes: Final Draft software, Syd Field's Screenwriting Video, select screenwriting magazine subscriptions, website development and promotions, professional script reviews, scholarships to the film festival's educational programs such as "ScriptBiz."

Success story: Last year, filmmaker/screenwriter Jonny Kurzman of London, England took Grand Prize with his *Night of Life*. He has since presented his work to BBC Channel 4 and is in negotiations.

> **"**Inexperienced writers commonly create dialogue replete with y'know, ummm, errr, hey, look, listen, I think, by the way, and a host of other hedges and thrust-blunting interjections.**"**
>
> —from *Screenwriting: The Art, Craft and Business of Film and Television* by Richard Walter

CAPE FOUNDATION NEW WRITER AWARD

Purpose:	To promote screenwriters of Asian or Pacific Islander heritage
Entry fee:	$35
Year began:	1999
Categories:	Best Screenplay
Sponsor:	Cape Foundation
Address:	P.O. Box 251855 Los Angeles, CA 90025
Fax:	(310) 278-2313
Email:	info@capeusa.org
Website:	www.capeusa.org (Rules, application, more.)
Deadline:	Autumn
Rules:	See website (New Writer Awards).
Best Advice:	Re-write and submit!
Director:	Cindy Sison
Judges:	Blue Ribbon Panel of studio and independent executives
Cash prizes:	$2,500
Non-cash prizes:	Writing software and opportunity to pitch to Blue Ribbon Panel.
Success story:	See comments from 1999 Winner Cynthia Liu on website.

CHESTERFIELD FILM COMPANY
SCREENWRITING FELLOWSHIP

Purpose:	To connect writers with the industry.
Entry fee:	$39.50
Categories:	Open to screenwriters, novelists and playwrights; any genre, any form.
Sponsor:	The Writer's Film Project, Paramount Pictures
Address:	Chesterfield Film Company Screenwriting Fellowship 1158 26th St. PMB 544 Santa Monica, CA 90403
Phone:	(213) 683-3977
Fax:	(310) 260-6116
Email:	info@chesterfield-co.com
Website:	www.chesterfield-co.com
Deadline:	November 9 (extended deadline)
Rules:	Submit one or two screenplays. Include a one-page synopsis, and a log line of no more than 3-4 sentences in length. (See website for more.)
Best advice:	Writers are evaluated on the basis of prose and dramatic writing samples. Interested writers may submit writing samples in a variety of forms. No particular type of sample has an advantage in the application process. Acceptance is based solely on storytelling talent, regardless of the genre.
Director:	Doug Rosen, Melissa Ardolina
Judges:	Industry experts
Cash prizes:	$20,000; up to five fellowships may be awarded.
Non-cash prizes:	One-year fellowship program based in Los Angeles.
Success story:	In the past three years, fifteen scripts written by WFP alumni have been produced. Alumni have written scripts for nearly every studio and major independent in Hollywood.

THE CHESTERFIELD EXPERIENCE

by Margo Katz

I submitted a two-act play both to the Chesterfield and the Disney fellowships as I was wrapping up my Master's Degree at Smith College. I had promptly forgotten about both contests and moved to Manhattan when I got a call from Chesterfield offering me a screenwriting fellowship.

I learned two valuable lessons from being a Chesterfield fellow:

If you don't have the innate talent of storytelling, the craft of screenwriting is a hollow, useless tool; and, having that innate talent means nothing unless you find an advocate who will market and exploit that talent.

I was one of the first ten recipients—most of us plucked from college and university writing programs. Real, raw talent. Much like Dorothy landing in the full-color land of Oz, we were like kids in a candy store with full run of Steven Spielberg's Amblin Entertainment on the Universal Studios lot.

We zipped around the historic Universal back lot in golf carts, attended private screenings (free candy and popcorn!) and parties thrown in our honor, and met Spielberg himself. People like Buck Henry, Nick Kazan and Warren Beatty came to speak to us. Our scripts were sent to the top agencies in the industry. And we were assigned professional screenwriters as mentors.

We were taught to believe that the sun rose and set on us and on our screenplays.

We worked hard, too. We wrote and rewrote under deadline. We spent grueling hours around a table critiquing our friends' screenplays and surviving our friends' critiques.

Chesterfield was, in essence, a screenwriting boot camp with perks.

Did Chesterfield prepare me to be a screenwriter outside of the cocoon of the fellowship? Not a chance. I wasn't prepared for the rejection, the duplicity, the backbiting or the shallowness of this big business industry. Nor was I warned that it's not about art and innate talent, it's about commerce and timing. I went in a virgin and came out a virgin, and only through painful post-fellowship trial and error did I realize the reality of landscape of the craft that had chosen me.

I wouldn't trade the Chesterfield experience for anything . . . except perhaps my soul and a two-picture deal.

CINESTORY SCREENWRITING AWARDS

Purpose:	To bring your writing to its next level—whether that's a three-picture deal or your next screenplay. We work in-depth with emerging screenwriters to hone their craft and help them find alternative access to the screen. We want to create a sustaining, nurturing community of writers who understand the professional demands of the craft, who can express their own voices through the medium, and who are trained to be collaborators with other filmmakers. Cinestory is a non-profit screenwriter's organization.
Entry fee:	Feature/Early: $40, Feature/Final: $50, Short/Early: $20, Short/Final: $25
Year began:	1996
Categories:	Features, Shorts, any genre.
Sponsor:	CineStory
Address:	CineStory Screenwriting Awards University of Chicago/Gleacher Center #36 450 N. Cityfront Plaza Dr. Chicago, IL 60611-4316
Phone:	(312) 464-8725 and (800) 6 STORY 6
Fax:	(312) 464-8724
Email:	cinestory@cinestory.com
Website:	www.cinstory.com (Awards, entry form, sponsors, success stories, rules, more.)
Deadline:	Early: September 15, Final: November 1
Rules:	Full-length feature film scripts; Short Film scripts 35 pages or less (see website for more).
Best Advice:	We reward originality and a strong personal voice. Write a script that will take the cinematic world by storm.
Director:	Pamela Pierce, Dona Cooper, co-founders
Judges:	Industry professionals

Cash prizes: $2,000.

Non-cash prizes: Three winners join the Mentorship Program for one year; script sessions, meetings, membership, script consultation with a leading cinematographer and a leading film editor, 2,000 feet of film to be used for production of the script, more; Semi-finalists receive discounts on script sessions, private reception, publicity, subscriptions, software, more.

Success story: Options, agency representation, readings.

TIPS

by Jim Mercurio, Hollywood Script Consultant

1. Scripts aren't novels. Think "movie," not "a good read."
2. Have one clear specific question and action in mind for your protagonist.
3. That question and action should be preceded by the hardest choice your protagonist has to make in the entire movie.
4. Structure and character are inexorably linked.
5. Except for ten screenplays in the history of the world, format, pacing, readability and page count affect reader's appreciation of the material.
6. Every subplot, character, scene, line of dialogue or word of action and description must contribute constructively to the script.
7. Message films are boring. But don't totally avoid theme. You get a couple of sentences within the first two-thirds of the script to shed partial light on the theme. Then you illuminate your theme completely in the climax of the film, with subplots that support that theme.
8. Cut. Edit.
9. Keep them wanting more.
10. Don't memorize this list.

COLORADO INDEPENDENT FILM FESTIVAL
AND SCREENWRITING CONTEST (CIFF)

Purpose:	To identify and nurture up-and-coming writing talent.
Entry fee:	$15
Categories:	Screenplays and treatments.
Sponsor:	SEG Films
Address:	CIFF P.O. Box 461164 Aurora, CO 80046-1164
Phone:	(303) 400-1525
Email:	segfilms@aol.com
Website:	www.segfilms.com
Deadline:	June 15
Rules:	Cannot be under option, sold or produced. (See website for more.)
Director:	Mark Sparks, President of Acquisitions
Judges:	SEG Films
Cash prizes:	Contact contest.
Non-cash prizes:	Writing assignments, software, more.

CREATIVECRIB.COM:
LARRY SUGAR MASTER CLASS

Purpose:	To connect promising writers and filmmakers with renowned industry professionals and produce successful entertainment properties. There are two parts to CreativeCrib: Education and Entertainment Production. Finalists will enroll in the Larry Sugar Master Class, an online course that teaches the essentials of producing. Based on "The Business of Education" course that Mr. Sugar teaches at the College of Santa Fe, where he is an adjunct professor, the master class provides an essential foundation for a career as a filmed entertainment producer.
Entry fee:	$60
Year began:	2000
Categories:	Film, Television, Music
Sponsor:	DCINEMA Entertainment, Inc.; No Equal Entertainment, INSINC, Screenplay Systems, *MovieMaker* magazine, *Scr(i)pt* magazine, Academy of Canadian Cinema and Television, Mosaic Media, Prospect Point, Rogers Video, Shaw.
Address:	DCINEMA ENTERTAINMENT INC. P.O. Box 28553 555 West Hastings Street Vancouver, B.C., V6B 4N4, Canada.
Fax:	(604) 605-1311
Email:	info@creativecrib.com
Website:	http://www.CreativeCrib.com
Deadline:	April 15
Rules:	Anyone may apply. You must submit a screenplay, teleplay or story treatment (no more than 140 pages), along with a cover letter (addressed to Larry Sugar), a resume (CV) and complete application.
Best Advice:	Believe in your work, be persistent and have perseverance!
Director:	Daniel Frankel, President and CEO (DCINEMA Entertainment, Inc.)

Judges: Larry Sugar and the CreativeCrib Review Committee (varies from year to year).

Cash prizes: TBA

Non-cash prizes: 12-month option on intellectual property, software (MovieMagic Screenwriter), magazine subscriptions (*Scr(i)pt magazine, MovieMaker* magazine), video rental and theatre gift certificates, professional industry consultations, editorial and media exposure and promotion, potential development funding, license agreements and pre-sales.

Success story: Previous Master Classes have produced successful working producers, writers and directors. This is the first time the class is available to the public via www.CreativeCrib.com.

> **"**Avoid static locations: offices, hotel rooms, park benches—characters sitting around talking to each other. Avoid entrances and exits unless they increase audience interest.**"**
>
> —from *Screenwriting Tricks of the Trade* by William Froug

> **"**Avoid bar scenes, coffee scenes, restaurant scenes, sitting scenes.**"**
>
> —from *Screenwriting 434* by Lew Hunter

CRIPPLE CREEK FILM FESTIVAL
SCREENPLAY CONTEST

Purpose:	To connect screenwriters to the industry.
Entry fee:	Early: $35, Final: $45
Categories:	All writers who have not received consideration of any kind for any script over $5,000. No pornography; all other genres accepted.
Sponsor:	Cripple Creek Film Festival
Address:	Cripple Creek Film Festival Screenplay Contest P.O. Box 219 400 W. Midland Ave. #232 Woodland Park, CO 80866
Phone:	(719) 686-9249
Email:	michaelherst@cripplecreekfilmfest.com
Website:	www.cripplecreekfilmfest.com
Deadlines:	Early: July 21, Final: August 7
Rules:	Include SASE for confirmation. Must own the rights to the script. No adaptations, multiple entries accepted. We recommend registering or copyrighting your material. No substitutions, 90-130 pages. Do not send original. Material will not be returned. Submit two title pages. The first should have only the title; separate title page should have contact information. Do not include author's name anywhere else in the script. Number pages correctly. Do not send additional material. Bind with brads, cover with card stock. Written in English.
Director:	Michael Herst
Judges:	Industry professionals
Cash prizes:	Grand prize: $500, first place: $300, second place: $150, third place: $50.
Non-cash prizes:	Possible representation, publicity.

CYCLONE PRODUCTIONS
SCREENWRITERS' PROJECT

Purpose:	To give writers the opportunity to begin a career in screenwriting. To encourage experienced and first-time writers.
Entry fee:	Early: $40, Standard: $45, Final: $50
Year began:	1994
Categories:	Features, Low Budget Feature Projects
Sponsor:	Cyclone Entertainment Group
Address:	Cyclone Productions, Screenwriters' Project P.O. Box 148849 Chicago, IL 60614-8849
Phone:	(773) 665-7600
Fax:	(773) 665-7660
Email:	cycprod@aol.com
Website:	www.cyclone-entertainment.com
Deadlines:	Early: July 1, Standard: August 1, Final: September 1
Rules:	One or two page synopsis. To receive application forms, send a business-size SASE and indicate Features or Low Budget Features. Or, you can fax us your request.
Best Advice:	Follow directions carefully. About 30 percent of the applicants are missing required materials. Keep writing. Sometimes the most avant-garde material is also the most appealing. Do not submit non-required materials. Do not call or drop by. Don't ever give up!
Director:	Lee Alan
Judges:	Cyclone Productions
Cash prizes:	$5,000 (at least three writers).
Non-cash prizes:	Possible production, development or option.

CYNOSURE SCREENWRITING AWARDS

Purpose:	To expand the scope of mainstream cinema by recognizing, developing and producing film scripts with distinctive and challenging screen roles for both women and minorities.
Entry fee:	Rolling: $35 (February 12); $45 (March 12); $55 (April 16)
Year began:	1999
Categories:	Female Protagonist and Minority Protagonist (if the script qualifies for both categories, the writer is asked to choose the one that best describes the overall spirit of the screenplay).
Sponsor:	Broadmind Entertainment
Address:	3699 Wilshire Blvd., Suite 850 Los Angeles, CA 90010
Phone:	(310) 855-8687
Fax:	(310) 543-9177
Email:	cynosure@broadmindent.com
Website:	www.broadmindent.com
Deadline:	February 12, March 12, April 16
Rules:	Open to all writers in any country. Scripts by multiple authors are accepted and awards, if given, will be divided equally among those writers. All writers must sign the entry/release form. Screenplays must not have been previously optioned, purchased or produced. More than one script may be submitted, provided that a signed entry/release from and application fee accompanies each submission. Screenplays must not have been previously optioned, purchased or produced. Scripts must be registered with the WGA or the U.S. Copyright Office. Scripts must de the original work of the applicant(s). If based upon adapted material not in the public domain, applicant(s) must attach a statement attesting to their rights to make such adaptations. Entries must be accompanied by a signed entry/release form, application fee, two title pages. The first title page should be attached to the script;

the second unattached title page should have title, author's name, address/phone number. The author's name should not appear anywhere on the script. Include a SASE for acknowledgement of receipt of submission. Screenplays must be in English only, and may be of any genre. Do not send originals; material will not be returned. Standard format, 90-130 pages, numbered, fastened with two or three brads, with card stock covers. No handwritten or faxed submissions will be accepted.

Best Advice: If your lead character is a woman *and* a minority, consider submitting your screenplay in the Minority category. The Minority category receives half as many submissions, though each category offers the same prize. Think "outside the box." We receive a lot of scripts about victimization and abuse, and while those stories certainly have their place in the world of storytelling, we are especially attracted to scripts about women and minorities who are, or who become, empowered. Or protagonists whose stories reflect aspects of the female and/or minority experience that we haven't already seen on the screen many times before. Surprise us, take bigger risks, make bolder choices.

Founders: Two directors: Andretta Hamilton and Jennifer Marquis

Judges: Panel of industry professionals from Los Angeles-based studios, production companies and agencies.

Cash prizes: Two $2,000 first prizes (one per category).

Non-cash prizes: Professional story notes, feedback.

TIPS

from Rick Edelstein (WGA,DGA)

Many screenplay teachers offer formulas about what has to happen in Act II, about the 'arc' and about the spine of the piece, ad infinitum, ad nauseam. (And they have not had a screenplay produced.) My suggestion is to ignore 'em all, including what an agent or producer says, "Works in the Market." For every rule there is an original movie that went its own way regardless of the "market." I offer three rules:

1) Write what's meaningful for you ("Follow your bliss," as Joseph Campbell often said).

2) Read screenplays of movies that you like for form and content.

3) Ignore these rules.

DAILY SCRIPT'S GET A LIFE
SCREENWRITING COMPETITION

Purpose:	To find quality material to submit to investors and producers.
Entry fee:	Early: $25, Final: $40
Year began:	2000
Categories:	Any genre. Short script contest (no longer than 20 pages), feature screenplays (90-140 pages)
Sponsor:	The Daily Script and Quality Filmed Entertainment
Address:	Daily Script's Get A Life Screenwriting Competition P.O. Box 18A-460 Los Angeles, CA 90018
Phone:	(323) 733-6243
Email:	dana@dailyscript.com
Website:	www.dailyscript.com/contribute/contest.html (FAQs, tips and tricks, survey, message board, more.)
Deadline:	December 1
Rules:	See website for submission, mailing, eligibility and legal guidelines for each category.
Best Advice:	Write a polished screenplay, in proper format. Professionalism comes first. We want to be captured and taken away to a new world. Write something that can touch us emotionally. (See website for tips and tricks.)
Director:	Dana Franklin, Coordinator
Judges:	Dana Franklin and a select group of Daily Script "employees."
Cash prizes:	Feature first place receives an amount equal to half of the entry fees up to $2,500; Short Script first place receives an amount equal to half of the entry fees up to $1,000.
Non-cash prizes:	Submitted to investors, producers, Daily Script T-shirt, reading.

DEER CREEK PRODUCTIONS
SCREENPLAY COMPETITION

Purpose: Deer Creek Productions Executive Producer J. Cox is a Vietnam Veteran involved in feeding, clothing and assisting veterans in any way possible. Mr. Cox and other producers (all Vietnam Veterans) at Deer Creek Productions feel that a screenplay contest will generate quality screenplays, while contributing to a worthy cause. All funds go to a charity to feed homeless people. Previous year competitions have helped purchase food and supplies to those in need and homeless. We will continue to promote our competition as long as people want to donate to a good cause.

Entry fee: $35

Year began: "Our contest began a couple years ago."

Categories: Any genre (see Best Advice below).

Sponsor: Deer Creek Productions

Address: Deer Creek Productions Screenplay Competition
30765 Pacific Coast Highway #143
Malibu, CA 90265

Phone: (310) 457-6648

Fax: (310) 589-9862

Email: deercreek@earthlink.net

Website: www.members.a2zsol.com/deercreek.html. (Rules, guidelines, business plans, financing, budgets, script analysis, marketing plans.)

Deadline: August 31 (see website for exceptions)

Rules: Non-documentary, 90-120 pages, industry format, 3-hole punched, brad fasteners, card stock covers. Only the title should appear on the cover; writer's name should *not* appear on the title page. More than one script per writer acceptable; each entry must be accompanied by the appropriate forms/fees. We strongly registration of material, must not have been sold or optioned at the time of submission, adhere to guidelines to avoid disqualification.

Best Advice:	Because the staff are mostly veterans, do not send war stories or military screenplays unless the story is well thought out, well researched and well written—these guys know the military and have turned away screenplays because of the phony material. A well-written screenplay speaks louder than anything else, but the stories that captivate our attention are those that rise to intensity, remain unique and generate a laugh and a tear.
Director:	Andrea Shelis, Administrator of Competition
Judges:	Established screenwriters and experienced producers
Cash prizes:	$250.
Non-cash prizes:	Certificate, development assistance, business plan, option consideration, possible production.

> **❝** Most readers read dialogue, while scanning the narrative . . . You have ten pages to grab their attention . . . In the very first page, any professional reader will get an immediate sense of the level of your writing. **❞**
>
> —from *Screenwriting Tricks of the Trade*
> by William Froug

DRAMA GARAGE THURSDAY NIGHT
SCRIPT READING SERIES

Purpose:	We focus on getting projects seen by people who can launch them. We are dedicated to finding and developing screenplays by bringing them life via a staged reading with actors. Part industry showcase, part workshop, part debut.
Entry fee:	$25
Year began:	1998
Categories:	Any genre. Keep in mind, sci-fi and action pieces that are description-heavy are hard to produce. Description-heavy thrillers are difficult as well. Pieces where acting ability is important seem to work the best.
Sponsor:	Working Pictures
Address:	1861 N. Whitley #205 Los Angeles, CA 90028
Phone:	(323) 993-5700
Email:	info@dramagarage.com
Website:	www.dramagarage.com
Deadline:	Once a month, call for schedule.
Rules:	Must be original. Not to exceed 120 pages. No first drafts and no shooting scripts. If your script is accepted, you may be asked to modify it to fit the format. Must be able to meet with a Drama Garage representative at least once before the reading. No material will be returned.
Best advice:	Too many scripts are formulaic and rehashed versions of what is already out there or has already been done many times. Give us a good story. That's all we look for. I don't care who is attached or how many awards it has won—if there is no story, there is no film. Limit the camera angles in the script.
Director:	Maryam Dalan, Executive Creator, Producer
Judges:	One reader who passes the recommended scripts on to a story editor who passes the final scripts to the Executive Creator/Producer.

Non-cash prizes: Eight to ten scripts a year are chosen to be done as live reads for an industry audience. The reading includes: A fully produced and staged screenplay reading at Occidental Studios in Hollywood; a cast of up to twelve professional actors to act out the script; a director; one rehearsal; space for an audience; beverage reception for up to 100 people; press release, contacts, software, more.

Success story: Development execs, producers or agents have contacted all writers who have had readings.

TIPS

from *Writing Short Films* by Linda J. Cowgill

STORYTELLING ELEMENTS
Hero, want, action, conflict, climax and resolution.

CHARACTER CONFLICT
The best characters are strong personalities who oppose each other over the story problem.

STORY AND PLOT
A plot is a series of carefully devised and interrelated actions, which progresses through a struggle of opposing forces to a climax and resolution.

OPENINGS
Good openings are visual, utilizing the language of the medium—images and sounds—to conjure feelings and carry the story's mood to the audience.

STRUCTURE
There is no set formula for writing a screenplay.

PLOTTING
Every good scene has one main plot the writer wants to communicate. Presenting too many points in one scene will create problems for the audience.

DIALOGUE
Always read your dialogue out loud. If the words and sentences are awkward or hard to speak, then it is ineffective screenplay dialogue.

EMPIRE SCREENPLAY CONTEST

Purpose:	To enhance the availability of quality material for Hollywood.
Entry fee:	Early: $40, Standard: $45, Final: $50
Year began:	1996
Categories:	Hollywood or Bust: relatively expensive to produce; High Value: relatively inexpensive to produce.
Sponsor:	Empire Screenplay Contest
Address:	Empire Screenplay Contest 12358 Ventura Blvd. #602 Studio City, CA 91604-9919
Phone:	(661) 420-9919
Email:	empirecontact@yahoo.com
Website:	www.geocities.com/empirecontact. (Submissions, promotion, judging, guidance, perspective)
Deadline:	Early: June 15, Standard: July 15, Final: August 15
Rules:	The process encourages resubmissions. Feature length scripts, no documentaries. (See website for specific submission rules.)
Best advice:	See website for initial submission, presentational advice; word-use advice for semi-final judging; content advice for final judging.
Director:	Michael J. Farrand, Administrator
Judges:	Hollywood producers
Cash prizes:	$2,000 each category.
Non-cash prizes:	Publicity, staged reading for the winning script in the High Value category.
Success story:	Sales, options, representation. (See website for more.)

EMPYRION PICTURES SCREENPLAY COMPETITION

Purpose: Whether your script is for big budget Hollywood movie or a quirky independent story, the mission of the Empyrion Pictures Screenplay competition is to promote and support talented new writers.

Entry fee: $35 (U.S.), late entry $45 (U.S.)

Year began: 2001

Categories: all genres accepted.

Sponsor: Empyrion Pictures

Address: Empyrion Pictures Screenplay Competition
#203 627-23 Ave SW
Calgary, Alberta, Canada T2S 0J6

Email: empyrion@telusplanet.net or
relvers_98@yahoo.com

Website: www.telusplanet.net/public/empyrion/

Deadline: April 1 or May 1 (late)

Rules: All entries must contain:

Completed entry form.

Entry fee in the form of a *Money Order payable to Empyrion Pictures*. (Canadian applicants *only* may remit in CDN funds or with a check.)

One copy of a completed feature-length screenplay (approx. 90-130 pages) in industry standard format. The script must have title page containing the title, author's name, address, email address and phone number. You may enter as many times as you wish, however, each entry must contain separate entry forms and applicable fees. Submission must be the original work of the author.

Submissions must be postmarked no later than April 1 (early deadline) or May 1 (late deadline). Applications are accepted only by mail and material cannot be returned by Empyrion Pictures.

The decisions of the judges are final and not subject to negotiation.

The names of applicants whose scripts have advanced to the next round of competition will be posted on the website by August 1, 2001 and will also be notified by mail of their status.

The winning applicant will be notified no later than September 1, 2001.

An award in the amount of $2,500 U.S. will be paid to the winning applicant.

Best Advice:	Don't send early drafts of a script. Film is a visual medium and stories need to be told visually, not through dialogue.
Director:	Richard Elvers
Judges:	Employees of Empyrion Pictures and other industry professionals in the Canadian and American independent film scene.
Cash prizes:	$2,500. (U.S.)
Success story:	Hopefully this year's winner!

> **❝** The premise of each second attributes to the premise of the minute of which it is part, just as each minute gives its bit of life to the hour, and the hour to the day. And so, at the end, there is a premise for every life in general. **❞**
>
> —from *The Art of Dramatic Writing*
> by Lajos Egri

EPICO PRODUCTIONS SCREENWRITING CONTEST

Purpose:	The selected screenplays will be produced by Epico Productions and will be distributed.
Entry fee:	No fee (All entrants must be members of EpicoEntertainment.com, which is $12.95 per month.)
Year began:	2001
Categories:	Any genre. Children's stories, books on tape.
Sponsor:	EpicoEntertainment.com
Email:	EpicoEntertainment.com—accepts submissions only through website.
Website:	EpicoEntertainment.com
Deadline:	December 30, 2001
Rules:	Must submit synopsis which should include locations and cast breakdowns.
Judges:	Staff of EpicoEntertainment.com
Cash prizes:	Winner will receive a percent of the net profits.
Non-cash prizes:	Your work will be produced and distributed.
Success story:	This is our first contest of many but check out our last film on our site EpicoEntertainment.com.

EUROSCRIPT/FILM STORY COMPETITION

Purpose:	Script development
Entry fee:	£25
Categories:	Feature films and TV
Sponsor:	Media Programme/European Union
Address:	Suffolk House 1-8 Whitfield Place London, England W1T 5JU
Fax:	44 20 7387 5880
Email:	euroscript@netmatters.co.uk
Website:	www.euroscript.co.uk
Deadline:	April 30, October 31
Rules:	This is a competition for the citizens of the European Union.
Best Advice:	A crisp, thrilling story.
Director:	Paul Gallagher
Judges:	Euroscript
Non-cash prizes:	Free script development.

❝Leave out editing, music, acting, casting and directing instructions.**❞**

—from *Screenwriting 434*
by Lew Hunter

FADE IN: SCREENWRITING AWARDS

Purpose:	To promote screenwriters
Entry fee:	$40
Year began:	1995
Categories:	Feature length or Shorts in categories of Comedy, Action/Adventure, Thriller, Drama, Film Noir.
Sponsor:	*Fade In* magazine
Address:	Fade In: Screenwriting Awards 289 S. Robertson Blvd #465 Beverly Hills, CA 90211
Phone:	(800) 646-3896
Email:	fadeinmag@aol.com
Website:	www.fadeinmag.com (Entry form, rules, finalists)
Deadline:	October 30
Rules:	Open to anyone. Work must not have been optioned at time of submission and must be the original work of author. May enter as many times as you wish, but one entry per application.
Best Advice:	Write something original.
Judges:	Agents, producers, executives
Cash prizes:	First place (each category): $500, second place (each category): $250, third place (each category): $100.
Non-cash prizes:	Grand prize: computer, expense paid trip (hotel and airfare, or cash equivalent to $1,000) to meet with top literary agents and studio executives for three days, two nights; first place (category): Waterman fountain pen, software, magazine subscription; second place (category): script analysis, magazine subscription; third place (category): script analysis, magazine subscription. Industry exposure.

FILM FLEADH SCREENPLAY COMPETITION

Purpose:	To showcase emerging Irish and Irish-American, and Irish-descent writers who have a unique voice.
Categories:	Favor Irish or Irish-American stories.
Entry fee:	$25
Year began:	1999
Sponsor:	Film Fleadh Festival
Address:	I.I.F.F. Screenplay Competition 29 Greene St. New York, NY 10013
Phone:	(212) 966-3030
Fax:	(212) 965-9520
Email:	filmfleadh@aol.com
Website:	www.filmfleadh.com
Deadline:	January 15
Rules:	Must not have been optioned, produced or sold. Must be written in English, 70-140 pages. Send two copies in proper format.
Best Advice:	Write something original, with a fresh voice. It does not have to be Irish themed (but it does help). Also, we favor scripts that give Ireland and its people a positive outlook or a new spin at looking at the Irish or Irish-American culture.
Director:	Cynthia O'Murchu, Festival Coordinator
Judges:	I.I.F.F.
Cash prizes:	Contact contest.
Non-cash prizes:	Publicity.

FILM IN ARIZONA
SCREENWRITING COMPETITION

Purpose:	To help a screenplay set in Arizona get attention from industry executives in a position to produce the screenplay—hopefully, in Arizona.
Entry fee:	Until April 15: $30; after April 15 until May 15: $40.
Year began:	1997
Categories:	All genres accepted.
Sponsor:	Past sponsors have included Southwest Airlines, Mondrian Hotel, Enterprise Car Rental, The Screenwriter's Room, Arizona Commission on the Arts, Writers Script Network, Cox Communications
Address:	Film in Arizona Screenwriting Competition 3800 N. Central Avenue, Bldg. D Phoenix, AZ 85012
Phone:	(602) 280-1380
Fax:	(602) 280-1384
Email:	wendyc@azcommerce.com
Website:	www.azcommerce.com/azfilmcommission.htm
Deadline:	May 15
Rules:	Eighty-five percent or more of screenplay must be set in Arizona. You do not have to be an Arizona resident to enter. Multiple entries accepted if each is accompanied by a separate application form and check. Writing teams permitted. Resubmission of scripts from past years is allowed. Must be the original, unpublished work by the contestant(s) and not sold or optioned at the time of submission (options that have expired are acceptable). Proper formatting, brass brads, professional presentation. Consult website for detailed rules and submission procedures.

Best Advice:	Because we're Arizona specific, many writers are frightened off, assuming the scripts must be travelogues or stories about space aliens or westerns. We welcome all genres. This smaller amount of submissions is terrific news for the writers as the competition is not overwhelming.
Coordinator:	Wendy Carroll, Special Projects Coordinator, Arizona Film Commission
Judges:	First and second round: Arizona film industry. Third round: Los Angeles film industry, overseen by George Kirgo, President of the Writers Guild Foundation.
Cash prizes:	$1,000 from Cox Communications to top-scoring screenplay. $1,000 from the Arizona Commission on the Arts for top-scoring Arizona writer among the finalists.
Non-cash prizes:	All finalists are flown to an Awards Breakfast in Los Angeles where they can break bread and rub shoulders with production company executives and literary agents. The Grand Prize Winner wins return airfare to Los Angeles from one of the sponsoring airlines hub cities, hotel accommodations, rental car, $1000 cash, optional free listing on Writers Script Network website, a sizeable congratulatory advertisement in both Daily Variety and Hollywood Reporter, and a script pitching session to prepare the winner for pre-arranged meetings with industry professionals who have agreed to read the winning script and meet with the writer. We consider this to be a foot-in-the-door prize package—everything the writer needs!

FILM COMMISSION SCREENPLAY CONTEST

by Wendy Carroll, Special Projects Coordinator "Film in Arizona" (Linda Peterson Warren, Director)

The Arizona Film Commission's "Film In Arizona" screenwriting contest is particularly close to my heart as, for many years, I taught screenwriting through seminars, workshops, private classes and as a guest speaker to writer's groups. Prior to that, I was a producer with Disney for thirteen years. During that time I also worked as a story analyst for Disney. I've been in the industry since 1980.

I have tried to stress to screenwriters the importance of presentation and format. Some writers don't feel format is worth worrying about—they feel their characters are so intense, their dialogue so sparkling, their story so exciting that they could write it in crayon on the back of a grocery bag and still sell it. Possible—like it's possible I could win the lottery. Why create reasons for readers and producers to expect less of your work? Some contests assign points for proper format. Others dismiss a script entirely if it's not formatted properly. I can always spot a writer who has copied format from a book or a production/shooting script. Even if the dialogue, characters and action are in the appropriate slots, there are other giveaways that the writer doesn't fully understand format. When I come across a script that is cleanly formatted, it's a delight—it certainly puts me in the right frame of mind to sit back and enjoy the read.

Regarding content, I'd say that easily 50 percent or more of the scripts submitted could fit into one category—repetitive story line. Enough already with retired cops, about-to-retire cops, crusty cops, rookie cops, rogue cops, cops bucking the system, cops in mourning for their deceased partners/spouses/children/ex-cop fathers. Too often, new writers try to rewrite the movie they saw last month; they just change the character names and alter the situations.

Running a screenplay contest is actually a lot of fun. It's exciting to watch the second rounders, finalists and, ultimately, the winner emerge.

FILMCONTEST.COM

Purpose:

To support new and exciting writers and help them connect with other people in the industry who can recognize and advance the writer's career.

Entry fee:

$40

Year began:

2000

Categories:

All genres accepted.

Sponsor:

The Filmmakers Collective

Address:

The Filmmakers Collective
1328 Broadway, Suite 1024-PMB #117
New York, NY 10001

Phone:

(212) 252-5303

Email:

info@filmcontest.com

Website:

www.filmcontest.com
(Forms, guidelines, awards, sponsors, more)

Deadline:

June 30 (2000 contest extended to July 31)

Rules:

English only, in industry standard format, between 80-160 pages, original work (WGA registration is suggested), bound with card stock cover page with title and author's name. Material will not be returned. Multiple entries are acceptable, but must be accompanied by the appropriate forms/fees. Cannot have been previously optioned or sold (see website for more).

Best Advice:

Be original! Write stories that push boundaries and grab attention from page one. Careful of the following: wrong format, misspellings, overuse of flashbacks and dream sequences, too many characters, too many camera directions.

Director:

James LaBudde, Coordinator

Judges:

First round judged by contest staff; second round judged by independent professional screenplay readers; final round of top ten judged by production professionals in the film industry.

Cash prizes:

$3,000.

Non-cash prizes: Paid trip to New York or Los Angeles for pitch meeting, publicity, notes, script read by at least five different production companies.

SCRIPT FORMAT: FOLLOW THE RULES FOR SUCCESS

by Tracy Clark, Managing Editor, *New York Screenwriter*

Nothing is more aggravating to readers than improperly formatted screenplays. Mistakes run the gamut from poor grammar, numerous typos and missing pages to huge blocks of text and excessive camera angles. Though script formatting computer programs on the market have improved conditions a great deal, many writers are still making costly errors that result in instant rejection.

"If it's a feature script, I'll know after the first twenty pages whether or not I want to read any further," admits agent Bruce Brown of Los Angeles.

"No camera angles," cautions Larissa Bills. "It makes it very confusing because we're only looking for a screenplay." It is the director's responsibility to come up with camera angles.

The story can get lost if the writer is overly concerned with the look of the film. Developing strong motivated characters, a compelling plot, and believable dialogue is difficult enough.

Too often writers believe that setting the opening scene means describing everything down to the finest detail. It is not unusual to find scripts that have the heaviest descriptive passages in the first ten pages. "I find that scripts that have overly long descriptive passages tend to look forbidding," admits producer Alex Rose. "Scripts should be clear and easy to read so that our eye can just move down the page quickly."

"For some reason I see a lot of this," says Rizzo, "openings where the writer starts out in prose and sort of segues into the standard format." Using prose without a slugline interchangeably with industry format is confusing and jarring. The writer should decide if he is writing a script or a novel.

The script should be bound with a heavy card stock cover and two 1 1/4-inch round head brass fasteners for the top and bottom holes. Any other binding method would be unacceptable and also considered the mark of an amateur.

Writers should invest in a top quality laser printer or ink jet printer. Dot matrix printers, unless they can produce letter quality type, should not be used.

FILMMAKERS.COM / THE RADMIN COMPANY SCREENWRITING COMPETITION

Purpose: To give the greatest number of aspiring screenwriters the opportunity to begin their journey and have their material read by a leading Hollywood agency.

Entry fee: $35 (March 1); $45 (June 30)

Year began: 2000

Categories: All

Sponsor: Media Pro Tech Inc. c/o FilmMakers.com

Address: Screenplay Division
                  P.O. Box 3489
                  Chatsworth, CA 91313-3489

Email: contest@filmmakers.com

Website: http://www.filmmakers.com/

Deadline: June 30

Rules: See website.

Best Advice: Believe, visualize and dreams become real!

Director: William Masterson

Judges: The Gersh Agency, Bender-Spink Management, Oak Island Films Inc., Cindy Cowan Entertainment, The Knight Company, Entertech Media Group Inc., IMMI Pictures

Cash prizes: $3,000.

Non-cash prizes: Top fifty scripts will be read by The Radmin Company, top five will be read by The Gersh Agency, Bender-Spink Management, Cindy Cowan Entertainment, etc. Free tuition to the Santa Fe Screenwriting Conference (SFeSC), Final Draft Screenwriting Software.

OFFICIAL RULES AND CONDITIONS

Filmmakers.com/The Radmin Company Screenwriting Competition

Please read this document carefully and thoroughly prior to entering the contest.

Eligibility

- Entry fee per screenplay is $35 (U.S.) if postmarked by March 1.
- Entry fee per screenplay is $45 (U.S.) if postmarked by June 30.
- This contest is open to anyone except all employees, directors, associates, the immediate families of FilmMakers.com and all of its affiliates and/or sponsors and The Radmin Company.
- ONLY THE TITLE OF THE SCRIPT SHOULD APPEAR ON THE FRONT COVER! The writer's name should not appear anywhere on the script but only on the Entry Form.
- Submissions must be full-length film or television movie scripts in any genre.
- Multiple entries are permissible, but each entry must be accompanied by a signed Entry Form and an entry fee.
- Adaptations from other works are permissible provided you have the writer's written permission to adapt the work.
- All writer's must sign the Entry Form.
- Writers under the age of 18 years old must have a parent or guardian sign the Entry Form.
- Contest applicants must accept without reservation the decisions rendered by the jurors.
- Collaborative work is eligible, but each must fill and sign the Entry Form individually. The writers are responsible for the distribution of the contest prize(s).
- The screenplay must not have been previously optioned, sold or produced.
- Applicant must not have received consideration in excess of $5,000 as a prize in a previous competition.

- You have retained at least one copy of the submitted material, and you understand that all material we receive cannot and will not be returned under any circumstances.
- You have the option to include a one page synopsis of your screenplay.
- Make your money order, bank check, credit card check (in U.S. funds only), payable to: Media Pro Tech Inc.

Submit all material together and send by mail to:

In U.S.A.	In Canada
FilmMakers magazine	FilmMakers magazine
2001 Screenplay Competition	2001 Screenplay Competition
P.O. Box 3489	P.O. Box 3666, M.P.O.
Chatsworth, CA 91313-3489	Vancouver, BC, V6B 3Y8
USA	Canada

Screenplay Format and Length
- Script must be in industry standard format, in English, bound with two or three brads, with card stock covers, and must be between 80-140 pages.

Contest Deadline
- All scripts must be postmarked by June 30.
- FilmMakers.com is not responsible for late or lost submissions.

Confirmation Receipt
- When your submission is received, you will be notified by E-mail only (within two weeks). So please provide an E-mail address.

Permission
- By entering this contest and in the event you are declared a finalist (top ten) and or winner, you understand and accept that we will be free to use your name and likeness for advertising or promotional purposes without additional consideration.
- You may simultaneously submit your screenplay to any other person, contest, producer, agent and or organization.
- Entering this contest will not limit your copyright in any way. You retain all rights to your property.

THE FINAL DRAFT INTERNATIONAL
SCREENWRITING COMPETITION

Purpose:	To give aspiring writers their Big Break.
Entry fee:	$45-55
Year began:	1999
Categories:	Open to all genres.
Sponsor:	Final Draft, Inc., Cannell Studios and Express.com
Address:	16000 Ventura Blvd. #800 Encino, CA 91436
Fax:	(818) 995-4422
Email:	info@finaldraft.com
Website:	www.finaldraft.com
Deadline:	varies
Rules:	Open to all writers, screenplays cannot be under current option.
Best Advice:	Send the work you are most proud of.
Director:	Final Draft, Inc.
Judges:	Top industry professionals
Cash prizes:	$10,000 distributed amongst the winners.
Non-cash prizes:	Yes.
Success story:	The winner of our first contest (1999), Ken Hastings, had his screenplay *Dawg* produced, starring Denis Leary and Elizabeth Hurley; scheduled for release in 2001.

FLICKS ON 66
"WILD WEST DIGITAL SHOOTOUT"

Purpose:	To invite ten finalists to come to Albuquerque, NM to shoot, edit and screen the movie made from their script.
Entry fee:	$35
Categories:	Script for short subject digital video movie.
Sponsor:	Flicks on 66
Address:	Flicks on 66 P.O. Box 7038 Albuquerque, NM 87194
Phone:	(505) 766-9414
Fax:	(888) 837-9289
Email:	info@FLICKSon66.com
Website:	www.FLICKSon66.com
Deadline:	April 1
Rules:	Open to original ten page scripts. Must have a cover page with name, address, phone number, email address and title of the script. Include a short statement on the content and style of the piece and the directorial vision. Include a resume/bio of the screenwriter and director and/or screenwriter/director. (See website for more.)
Director:	Dennis Gromelski, Coordinator
Judges:	Flicks on 66
Non-cash prizes:	Digital video camera and editing equipment.

GVSU ANNUAL INTERNATIONAL
SHORT SCREENPLAY COMPETITION

Purpose: To find a screenplay that can be produced in our
                    summer film program.

Entry fee: None

Year began: 1994

Categories: Short scripts up to 30 minutes

Sponsor: Grand Valley State University

Address: Grand Valley State University
                    School of Communications
                    Allendale, MI 49401

Fax: (616) 895-2700

Email: philbinj@gvsu.edu

Website: www.gvsu.edu

Deadline: December 1st

Rules: Submit screenplay and one-page synopsis.

Best Advice: Good story/characters/ending.

Director: John Harper Philbin

Judges: GVSU faculty

Cash prizes: $300.

Non-cash prizes: We will produce the script!

Success story: East Lansing Film Festival (www.elff.com)
                    Winner Joe Piscatella went on to write and produce
                    for television. (See following)

SUCCESS STORY

by Joe Piscatella, winner,
Green Valley State Short Screenplay Competition

The name of my script that won the GVSU Short Screenplay Competition was *Survival of the Fattest*. The way the contest works is that the summer film program at Grand Valley State University produces the winning script. My script won, was produced and then publicly viewed. The director is looking to take it on the film festival circuit.

I received feedback on the script from the head of the film school. Based on his notes, I did three re-writes to get the script ready to shoot.

A management group in Los Angeles contacted the film school for a list of winners. I met with that company several times, but ultimately opted to sign with a different agency. Since winning the contest, I have written and produced episodes for NBC's *Stark Raving Mad*. I recently wrote a television special that will be used to promote the feature film *Shadow of the Vampire*. While these achievements are not directly related to my winning the GVSU competition, having something produced was definitely a boost for my confidence and resumé.

HOLLYWOOD SCREENPLAY CONSULTANTS
SCREENWRITING COMPETITION

Purpose: To find quality scripts for Hagan Productions.

Entry fee: $75

Year began: 1995

Categories: Open to all writers. Any genre. Low budget (less
                    than $1.5 million), character or story driven feature
                    film screenplays.

Sponsor: Hagan Productions and Cine-Vision 2000 Film and
                    Television Distribution Co.

Address: Hollywood Screenplay Consultants
                    17216 Saticoy St. #303
                    Van Nuys, CA 91406

Phone: (818) 994-5977

Email: Dhagan1393@aol.com

Website: www.swiftsite.com/Cine-Vision2000.
                    (Winners, what are we looking for, testimonials,
                    rules, more)

Deadline: March 1, June 1, September 1, December 1

Rules: Must not have been sold, optioned, be in turn-
                    around or produced at time of submission. Live
                    action, one or two locations is ideal, no more than
                    ten characters, 90-120 pages. No period pieces
                    (before 1985), no stunts, no special effects, no
                    famous music, no vampire stories.

Best Advice: Find out what we are looking for and submit that.

Director: Dave Calloway, VP Development

Judges: Dave Calloway, David Hagan

Cash prizes: First place: $2,000; second place: $1,000;
                    third place: $500.

Non-cash prizes: Possible option or purchase.

HOLLYWOOD SCREENPLAY DISCOVERY AWARDS

Purpose: To discover emerging screenwriters.

Entry fee: $55

Year began: 1990

Categories: Completed feature screenplays.

Sponsor: Hollywood Film Festival

Address: 433 N. Camden Drive, Suite 600
                   Beverly Hills, CA 90210

Fax: (310) 475-0193

Email: awards@hollywoodawards.com

Website: hollywoodawards.com

Deadline: Monthly. Yearly deadline is December 1st.

Rules: Unproduced screenplays only.

Best Advice: Know all about what you are writing and keep on
                   re-writing, re-writing and re-writing until you
                   believe the screenplay is ready to be shown.

Director: Carlos de Abreu

Judges: Hollywood executives—producers, actors and
                   agents.

Cash prizes: First place: $2,000; second place: $1,000;
                   third place: $500.

Non-cash prizes: VIP passes to the Hollywood Film Festival (valued at
                   $1,400).

Success story: Some of our finalists have found agents and gotten
                   writing jobs while others have had their scripts
                   optioned by producers and/or studios.

HOLLYWOOD'S SYNOPSIS WRITING CONTEST

Purpose: See website, "Why a Synopsis Competition?"

Entry fee: $20

Year began: 2000

Categories: All genres accepted.

Sponsor: Source World Wide Scriptservice

Address: Source World Wide Scriptservice
                   Synopsis Writing Contest, Head Office, Level 1
                   94 Hargrave Street
                   Paddington N.S.W. 2021
                   Sydney, Australia

Phone: 61-2-9326-1344

Fax: 61-7-5538-4465

Email: info@thesource.com.au

Website: www.thesource.com.au
                   (Submitting, tips, rules, sample, deadlines,
                   questions, winners)

Deadline: Last day of each month.

Rules: No longer than one page in length.

Best Advice: Double check all application details before
                   submitting. Keep it less than one page in length.

Directors: Allan Hawley Jacobs, Australia; Michael Carey,
                   Los Angeles

Judges: The Source World Wide Scriptservice

Cash prizes: Check website.

Non-cash prizes: Check website.

HOLLYWOODSCRIPT.COM HOTLIST

Purpose:	About every three months we choose the two best and most marketable screenplays from those with which we work.
Entry fee:	None, but must be consultation clients. (Consultation fee: $175)
Year began:	1999
Categories:	Screenplays, all genres.
Address:	See website.
Email:	craig.kellem@valley.net
Website:	hollywoodscript.com
Deadline:	next: March 10 and June 29
Rules:	See website.
Best Advice:	We do very effective consulting work. The contest is a free bonus.
Judges:	Craig Kellem, Judy Kellem
Non-cash prizes:	Will create free coverage which we guarantee will be read by a Hollywood agency.
Success story:	New(ish) contest. Five winners so far. Several are experiencing exciting marketing developments as a result of winning.

"Never write dialogue just for the sake of having small talk. There is no purpose for small talk.**"**

—from *Blueprint For Writing: a Writer's Guide To Creativity, Craft and Career* by Rachel Friedman Ballon, Ph.D.

HONG KONG TO HOLLYWOOD
SCREENPLAY CONTEST

Purpose: To capture the essence of Hong Kong.

Entry fee: none

Year began: 2000

Categories: Action, Drama, Romance—Treatments only

Sponsor: Hong Kong Tourist Association/Hong Kong
                   Film Services Office

Address: Hong Kong Tourist Assoc./Film Services Office,
                   10940 Wilshire Blvd. #2050,
                   Los Angeles, CA 90024

Email: writerscontest@htka.org

Website: www.discoverhongkong.com/usa/contest

Deadline: February

Rules: Treatments only, one to three pages (single sided).
                   Must be in English. Include: name, address, contact
                   numbers, email address. Must be original work,
                   must not have won previous awards; submissions
                   will not be returned. Recommend registration with
                   WGA.

Best advice: Capture the spirit of Hong Kong, the "City of Life,"
                   its romance, history, art, culture, heritage and peo-
                   ple; be creative, original and clear.

Judges: Minimum of three industry experts.

Cash prize: None.

Non-cash prize: 6 day/7 night trip for two to Hong Kong; meetings
                   with studio executives.

HORIZONS

Purpose:	To give new writers exposure in the industry.
Entry fee:	$35
Categories:	Unknown, unpublished, unproduced authors.
Sponsor:	Magnetic Media
Address:	Horizons 1130 N. Broadway North Massapequa, NY 11758
Phone:	(516) 783-8428
Email:	editor@wmpublishing-horizons.com
Website:	www.wmpublishing-horizons.com
Deadline:	September 30
Rules:	Unproduced screenplays. Rights remain with author. (See website for more.)
Director:	Steve Mena, Senior Editor
Judges:	WM Publishing
Cash prizes:	See website.
Non-cash prizes:	Publicity, publication, software.

> **"** The structure should not call attention to itself, nor should it be followed too precisely. The needs of the story dictate its structure. **"**
>
> —from *The Writer's Journey*
> by Christopher Vogler

IGOTTASCRIPT.COM

Purpose:	To get your script into the right hands in Hollywood.
Entry fee:	Early: $66, Final: $82
Year began:	2000
Category:	Any writer, feature length scripts.
Sponsor:	igottascript.com
Address:	igottascript.com 7095 Hollywood Blvd. #1380 Hollywood, CA 90028-8903
Phone:	(323) 860-6687
Email:	info@igottascript.com
Website:	www.igottascript.com (Purpose, contacts, entry forms, awards, more)
Deadline:	Early: July 28, Final: September 1
Rules:	Copyrighted or registered original work. Cannot have been previously optioned, sold or produced. Multiple writers acceptable. Multiple entries acceptable. No substitutions or corrected drafts. In English, 80-140 pages, bound with 2-3 brads, numbered pages.
Director:	Peter Soby Jr., Co-Coordinator
Judges:	igottascript.com
Cash prizes:	$1,000.
Non-cash prizes:	Round-trip airfare from anywhere in the world to Hollywood, limo service to and from airport, five days, four nights in Hollywood, meetings.

ILLINOIS/CHICAGO
SCREENWRITING COMPETITION

Purpose:	To promote local writing talent and promote the state/city as a film location.
Entry fee:	$25
Year began:	1996
Categories:	Feature films
Sponsor:	Illinois/Chicago Film Offices
Address:	IC Screenwriting Competition 1 North LaSalle #2165 Chicago, IL 60602
Phone:	(312) 814-8711
Fax:	(312) 814-8874
Email:	tlizak@commerce.state.il.us
Website:	www.commerce.state.il.us
Deadline:	Contest is biennial, no contest in 2001; check website for contest in 2002.
Rules:	100-125 pages, past winners not accepted, original work, cannot be previously produced or sold, must be copyrighted or registered, 75 percent must be set in locations filmable in Illinois, Illinois residents 18 and older.
Best Advice:	Follow the rules exactly. Submit your best work.
Director:	Todd Lizak, Co-coordinator
Judges:	Three tier system: Round one narrows the competition to fifty, round two narrows it to ten, round three determines three winners. IC staff and industry professionals
Non-cash prizes:	Submitted to a select group of studio executives and producers.

KARAOKE SOAPS MARATHON COMPETITION

Purpose: To create a viable and respectable writers lifeline to the broadcasting and theater industry.

Entry Fee: Registration fee is $5 U.S.; a script-processing fee of $2.50 per script keeps the program self-supporting.

Categories: Scripts need only be 17 to 19 minutes of dialogue and action. That's easy!

E-mail: michael_anthony@zenopierremediaworks.com

Website: http://www.zenopierremediaworks.com

Deadline: Monday, March 19. Don't wait for the last minute.

Best advice: This is a major career move disguised as a contest. It's fun! Writers are to write scripts of any category. The scripts are produced and then broadcast on AT&T Broadband and Time Warner Cable companies.

Director: Michael Anthony, Business Manager

Cash prizes: $75 U.S. is awarded weekly per script; two scripts will be accepted each week; sixteen weeks in all. That's a total of thirty-two scripts that will be selected, produced, broadcast and financially rewarded. Copyright safeguards are in place.

Non-cash prizes: The Ayo Awards Show and Dinner, will announce winners in the categories of Best Writer, Best Producer, Best Director, Best Actor, Best Supporting Actor and Best Singer following the competition. The awards show will also be produced and broadcast on the air.

KAY SNOW WRITING AWARDS

Purpose:	To encourage writers of the Northwest.
Entry fee:	$10 for members of Willamette Writers, $15 non-members. (No fee for 18 and under writers.)
Year began:	1976
Categories:	Open to anyone, any subject, short screenplays or partial scripts, 10 pages or less; Student Writer (18 or under), same rules apply.
Sponsor:	Willamette Writers
Address:	Kay Snow Writing Awards Willamette Writers 9045 SW Barbur Blvd. #5A Portland, OR 97219
Phone:	(503) 452-1592
Fax:	(503) 452-0372
Email:	wilwrite@willamettewriters.com
Website:	www.willamettewriters.com (Rules, guidelines, deadlines, release, more)
Deadline:	May 15
Rules:	See website.
Best Advice:	We suggest you enter the first ten pages. Find a strong, visual, interesting way to set a story into motion from the start. Find a way to engage the interest of an audience from page one, line one.
Director:	Cynthia Whitcomb, President
Judges:	Film industry professionals.
Cash prizes:	First place: $300, second place: $150, third place: $50. Student first: $50 (each age division).
Non-cash prizes:	Awards banquet, publicity.
Success story:	Options, representation.

KING ARTHUR SCREENWRITERS AWARD

Purpose:	Dedicated to working with new, untried writing talent as well as with established professionals.
Entry fee:	$55
Year began:	1997
Categories:	Open to anyone. All genres accepted.
Sponsor:	Kingman Films
Address:	KASA c/o *Scr(i)pt* magazine 5638 Sweet Air Rd. Baldwin, MD 21013
Phone:	(410) 592-3466
Fax:	(410) 592-8062
Email:	info@kingmanfilms.com
Website:	www.kingmanfilms.com
Deadline:	No set date for next contest. Check the website for updates.
Rules:	Scripts are not returned, multiple entries allowed, must be in industry format. (See website for more.)
Best Advice:	Proper professional format. We suggest you register your material. Include a clear one-page synopsis. Send only a copy of the script; do not send extraneous materials.
Director:	Contact contest.
Judges:	Kingman Films
Cash prizes:	$1,000,000 distributed among up to ten winners.
Non-cash prizes:	Production of the screenplay.

KLASKY CSUPO SCRIPTWRITING COMPETITION

Purpose:	To find far-out writers for the teen and/or adult markets.
Entry fee:	None
Year began:	2000
Categories:	Teen and/or adult market original animation teleplay. "Kid-appropriate" category in 2001.
Sponsor:	Klasky Csupo Productions
Address:	Klasky Csupo Scriptwriting Competition 6353 Sunset Blvd. Attn: Writers Competition Los Angeles, CA 90028
Phone:	(323) 468-3030
Email:	writerscompetition@klaskycsupo.com
Website:	www.klaskycsupo.com (Submission form, prizes, criteria.)
Deadline:	November 18
Rules:	Open to all writers. Submit one original animation teleplay for a 7-minute episode (no longer than 12 pages in length), in standard screenplay format. Each submission should feature original characters and give a general idea of the scope of the series. Submit a short synopsis of the overall concept and specific episode, along with brief character descriptions of all main characters (no longer than two pages). Script should include no more than 3-5 strong protagonists and be broadcast appropriate. Material will not be returned. Material becomes the property of Klasky Csupo.
Director:	Michael Faulkner, Director of Creative Affairs
Judges:	Klasky Csupo executives. Judging Criteria: originality, creativity, story idea, strength of character development.
Cash prizes:	First place: $5,000; second place: $2,500; third place: $1,500; five runner's up: $1,000 each.
Non-cash prizes:	Publicity.

N/G

LA FILMS INTERNATIONAL
SCREENPLAY COMPETITION

Purpose:	To identify and support screenwriters with extraordinary writing skills. We hope to help them market their best screenplays to producers, agents, production companies and studios.
Entry fee:	$40
Categories:	Open to everyone around the world, all genres.
Sponsor:	LA Films International
Address:	LA Films International Screenplay Competition P.O. Box 29190 Los Angeles, CA 90029-0190
Email:	omega@peachnet.campuscwix.net
Website:	www.lafylm.com
Rules:	Scripts not previously produced, sold or optioned, in English, 80-150 pages, proper format.
Director:	Judy Cummings, Contest Coordinator
Judges:	LA Films International
Cash prizes:	First place: $3,000; second place: $2,000; third place: $1,000; honorable mention: $200.
Non-cash prizes:	Publicity, industry contacts.

❝Villains must be extraordinary opponents.**❞**

—from *Television and Screenwriting:*
From Concept To Contract
by Richard A. Blum

LAUGHING HORSE PRODUCTIONS
SCREENPLAY CONTEST

Purpose:	To give unique and exciting scripts the attention they deserve.
Entry fee:	$45
Year began:	1997
Sponsor:	Laughing Horse Productions
Address:	Laughing Horse Productions P.O. Box 58023 Seattle, WA 98138
Phone:	(206) 762-5525
Fax:	(206) 768-9778
Email:	lhprods@yahoo.com
Website:	www.geocities.com/lhprods. (Prizes, guidelines/rules, entry form, more)
Deadline:	April 30
Rules:	Standard screenplay format, must be copyrighted or registered, include entry/release form.
Best Advice:	Write a script with compelling dialogue and unique characters. Write a script that is easy to visualize. Don't be afraid to take chances.
Director:	Alexia Wellons
Judges:	Laughing Horse Productions producers
Cash prizes:	First place: Memorial Scholarship, $1,000; second place: Memorial Scholarship, $500.
Non-cash prizes:	Readings in Los Angeles and Seattle.

LONE STAR SCREENPLAY COMPETITION

Purpose: To identify talented new writers and promote state
                    film production.

Entry fee: Students: $30, Early: $40, Final: $50

Year began: 1996

Categories: 1) Best script written by a writer from Texas;
                    2) Best non-Texas script;
                    3) Best gay/lesbian themed script;
                    4) Best script suitable for filming in Texas;
                    5) Best student script.

Sponsor: PB Productions, Irving Texas Film Commission

Address: Lone Star Screenplay Competition
                    1920 Abrams Pky. #419
                    Dallas, TX 75214-3915

Phone: (972) 606-3041

Email: lonestar@pic.net

Deadline: November 15

Rules: You may submit in each category. Include a three
                    sentence synopsis. (Contact contest for more.)

Best Advice: Enter early and follow the rules.

Judges: Industry professionals.

Cash prizes: First place: $300; second place: $50.

Non-cash prizes: Possible option, publicity, readings.

MARCO ISLAND FILM FESTIVAL

Purpose:	To recognize and honor independent filmmakers whose works touch our hearts and open our minds to the virtue of artistic expression.
Entry fee:	$20
Year began:	1998
Sponsor:	Collier County Tourist Development Council, MediaOne, the *New York Times*, SunTrust, Visitors Television Channel 39, Marco Island Eagle, Marco Movies, Arvida Realty Services, WSKB-FM
Address:	601 E Elkcam Circle B-6 Marco Island, Florida 34145
Fax:	(941) 394-1736
Email:	info@marcoislandfilmfest.com
Website:	marcoislandfilmfest.com
Deadline:	August 1
Rules:	Screenplays must be original works and include cover sheet with brief plot summary.
Director:	Pat Berry
Non-cash prizes:	Audience Awards

MARK ZIFCAK'S LOGLINE CONTEST

Purpose:	To give writers with finished scripts the opportunity to receive free script analysis; prepare them to sell their script.
Entry fee:	None
Year began:	2000
Categories:	All genres, all subjects, all writers.
Sponsor:	Mark Zifcak
Address:	Mark Zifcak's Logline Contest 508 S. Serrano Ave. #407 Los Angeles, CA 90020
Phone:	(909) 685-3689
Fax:	(815) 366-2812
Email:	mzifcak@lycos.com
Website:	http://mzifcak.tripod.com (Rules, examples (see following), about the sponsor, FAQs)
Deadline:	The end of every month.
Rules:	Must have a finished full-length feature film script for each logline. Email title, logline and the first ten pages of the completed script. You may remain anonymous. (Loglines are not protected by copyright, so don't enter if you don't want others to read it online.) Sponsor retains no rights to the material. Submit as many loglines as you have completed scripts. For feature stories only—no television pilots, MOWs, sitcoms or shorts.
Director:	Mark Zifcak, script analyst
Judges:	Mark Zifcak. Loglines are judged on conciseness and dramatic premise with the emphasis on compelling stories. Loglines will be judged first, then the first ten pages will be used to determine the winners.
Prizes:	Up to ten writers receive free script analysis.

MARK ZIFCAK'S LOGLINE CONTEST FAQs

How Does It Work?

Two feature film screenplays are chosen per month by their loglines. Submit your title and logline via email to mzifcak@lycos.com and the top loglines get their scripts read. It's that simple.

Who Is Eligible?

Anyone who has completed a feature film script and wants to do a rewrite.

What Does It Cost?

Nothing. This contest is absolutely free.

Loglines will be judged according to conciseness and dramatic premise with an emphasis on compelling stories.

The logline does not have to be "high concept," mainstream or complex. For instance: "Blind boy sets out across town to find his lost dog" will beat "Good versus Evil set in a faraway galaxy" (even though the second may have more cinematic value or be a more exciting story). A straightforward and concise logline is preferred to a vague and ultimately meaningless one.

Loglines will be judged according to the ability to make the reader want to read the script. If it's an action story, you should be able to see how this story will generate big action scenes. If it's a comedy, you should see the funny situations develop out of the concept. Try to intrigue the reader.

The Next Steps

After the scripts are chosen, each person will submit a hard copy of their script for review. I will analyze it and return notes on structure, character, plot and formatting. When a rewrite is completed, the script can be returned again for another free critique.

Time Limits

Notes will be returned in a timely fashion in the order the script material was received. I expect the rewritten script to be returned within a reasonable period of time if you want another critique. I have not determined the time frame but I expect it to be from two to three months.

Why Is This Offered For Free?

I always remembered J. Michael Straczynski saying that you should always give back. He gives generously to the writing community, even while creating and producing *Babylon 5* and writing television shows such as *Murder, She Wrote; Jake and the Fatman, The New Twilight Zone* and *The Real Ghostbusters*. Now I am in a position to help fellow writers and have chosen this method to give something back.

My Qualifications

My main script reading education began as a reader for the Scriptwriters Network Producers Outreach Program (under the tutelage of Jim Shea of the Producers Outreach Program) and the Carl Sautter contest. After critiquing scores of scripts and reading every screenwriting book I could get my hands on, I learned about stories and how they were put together.

The Fine Details

All winning loglines and critiques will be posted on this site along with periodic progress reports. Do not submit your logline if you don't want anyone else to see it; ideas are free and not protected by copyright!

I retain no rights to any of the written material submitted but retain the right to show examples of my critiquing with short excerpts of material being considered. This will hopefully benefit others who visit this site. By entering this contest, winners agree to let me post their name, loglines, and my critique of their material.

All logline submissions will be accepted via the Internet. The logline must be in the body of the email to be considered.

My critiques will be fair, impartial, objective—and most of all—constructive. I intend to help writers become better at what they do.

When does the next contest start?

Contests are now monthly.

When does it end?

Submissions will be accepted until the end of each month and winners chosen the first week of the following month.

How many writers win?

Two per month.

My idea is so good, I don't want anyone to steal it. Can I still send it in?
Your title and logline may be posted on this site for everyone to see. Better to send in one that you don't mind being publicized.

If I win, will you help me get an agent or sell my script?
I will only critique your story; the rest is up to you.

Can I send in the same entry next time?
Yes, but since it didn't get chosen the first time, perhaps you should rewrite it for the next round.

How many entries can I submit?
I will accept as many entries as completed scripts. If you have ten finished scripts, I will accept ten submissions. You may submit all loglines and pages in one email.

Can I enter my TV script?
This competition is for feature stories only. TV pilots or MOWs are not eligible. Full-length scripts for cable movies (since they are identical in structure to feature stories) are acceptable.

For more information or details on how to submit your entry, send email to mzifcak@lycos.com.

MASSACHUSETTS FILM OFFICE
ANNUAL SCREENWRITING COMPETITION

Purpose:	To promote statewide filming
Entry fee:	None
Year began:	1995
Categories:	Open to all writers, all genres.
Sponsor:	Massachusetts Film Office
Address:	Massachusetts Film Office Annual Screenwriting Competition 10 Park Plaza #2310 Boston, MA 02116
Phone:	(617) 973-8800
Fax:	(617) 973-8810
Email:	film@state.ma.us
Website:	www.state.ma.us/film. (Rules, judging criteria, more)
Deadline:	Contact contest.
Rules:	Eighty-five percent of the script's locations must be authentic Massachusetts locations. Submit two bound copies of an original story, 90-130 pages, in English. Industry format. Include application form. No substitutions after submission has been made. One script per writer or team. Use card stock covers, correctly numbered pages. The script title may appear on the upper right corner of each page. Do not send additional materials. No adaptations. Submissions from previous year are not eligible for current year.
Best Advice:	Follow all directions closely. Develop the story within the first fifteen pages. Scripts are evaluated on authenticity of locations, originality, structure, character development, dialogue, commercial potential and overall impression.
Director:	Robin Dawson

| Judges: | Los Angeles and Massachusetts film professionals. The first and second rounds will be judged by Massachusetts film, video and television professionals. Top five scripts advance to finals, judged by Los Angeles-based entertainment industry professionals. |
| Non-cash prizes: | Round-trip airline ticket to Los Angeles, three-night stay, publicity, meetings. |

> **"**Identification with a character means that the audience experiences emotion through that character. In other words, the audience puts itself inside the character emotionally to experience the story. If the character is in danger, the audience feels frightened; if the character suffers loss, the audience feels sad. You must employ at least one of the following methods to establish identification for your hero: Create sympathy for the characters; put the characters in jeopardy; make the character likable.**"**
>
> — from *Writing Screenplays That Sell* by Michael Hauge

MAUI WRITERS CONFERENCE
SCREENWRITING COMPETITION

Purpose:	To offer exposure to professionals in film and television industries.
Entry fee:	Early: $40, Final: $50
Year began:	1998
Categories:	Feature film screenplays
Sponsor:	Maui Writers Conference
Address:	Maui Writers Conference Screenwriting Competition Attn: Shawn Guthrie 4821 Lankershim Blvd. Suite F, #241 North Hollywood, CA 91601
Email:	mauiscript@aol.com
Website:	www.mauiwriters.com (Rules, application, release form, checklist, more)
Deadline:	Early: April 15, Final: June 1
Rules:	Complete the application/release forms. Standard format, minimum 85 pages, bound by three brads. No episodic television screenplays. Send two copies of the script. The title page should have only the title. A separate unbound title page should have the title, author's name, address/phone number. Write the title in black, in large block letters on the spine. We advice registering your material. Must include a SASE for verification that script has been received. Scripts will not be returned.
Best Advice:	Write well, write intelligently and tell a good story.
Director:	Shawn Guthrie, Coordinator
Judges:	Top agents, management companies, production companies, networks and studio representatives.
Cash prizes:	First place: $2,500; second place: $1,000; third place: $500.
Non-cash prizes:	Top three winners get paid admission to the Writers Conference.

MONTEREY COUNTY FILM COMMISSION
SCREENWRITING COMPETITION

Purpose:	To bring awareness of Monterey County to screenwriters and production personnel; to expose the judges to area locations; to raise funds for the nonprofit County Film Commission.
Entry fee:	Early: $40, Final: $50
Year began:	1997
Categories:	Feature film or television movie scripts.
Sponsor:	Monterey County Film Commission
Address:	Monterey County Film Commission P.O. Box 111 Monterey, CA 93942-0111
Phone:	(408) 646-0910
Fax:	(408) 655-9244
Email:	mryfilm@aol.com
Website:	www.tmx.com/mcfilm
Deadline:	Early: December 10, Final: December 31
Rules:	90-130 pages, multiple submissions accepted. Contest is limited to the first 500 screenplays received. Write for more information.
Best Advice:	Make the first 10-15 pages riveting. Use standard screenplay format.
Director:	Julie Armstrong, Film Commission Director
Judges:	Producers, agents, writers
Cash prizes:	First place: $1,000; second place: $500; third place: $250.
Non-cash prizes:	First through third place receive contacts, event, consultations, publicity; Fourth through sixth place gain recognition

MOONDANCE FILM FESTIVAL CONTESTS

Purpose: To promote women writers and filmmakers to the international film industry; to encourage, inspire and motivate films and writings by men and women depicting non-violent conflict resolution; to motivate men and women writers and filmmakers to depict women and girls in a positive manner and to write lead roles for women over forty; to encourage and reward young filmmakers 18 or younger.

Entry fee: $25, $50 and $75

Year began: 1999

Categories: Feature Screenplays, Short Screenplays, Stage Plays, Feature Films, Short Films, Documentary Films, Animation Films, TV Episodics, TV Pilots, TV Mows, Radio Plays, Musical Scores, Lyrics and Librettos, Music Videos

Sponsor: Egg Pictures, Final Draft, Gruenberg Pictures, WritersScriptNetwork.com, MovieBytes.com and others

Address: 970 Ninth Street
Boulder, CO 80302 USA

Email: moondanceff@aol.com

Website: www.moondancefilmfestival.com

Deadline: July 1 and October 1

Rules: See website for rules and eligibility requirements.

Best Advice: In all genres of writing and in all genres of film entries, have a *story*. A good story; a unique story or one that is told well, and which has interesting characters and great dialogue. Write visual stories for film.

Director: Elizabeth English

Judges: Elizabeth English, Linda Seger, Susie Conklin, Larry Brody and others

Non-cash prizes: Sterling silver mermaid pendant for Spirit of Moondance, Columbine Award, Seahorse Award, Dolphin Award.

Success story:	Scripts by Moondance winners have been purchased by Coppola and others, films purchased by Oxygen Media and others, Oscar® buzz for a winning documentary from Israel.
Notes:	Moondance has traditionally been a women-only competition, but in response to popular request, starting in 2001, we encourage both men and women writers and filmmakers to enter the special side-bar competition, The Seahorse Contest. To be eligible for the Seahorse competition, submissions of films and screenplays, stageplays, radio scripts, TV scripts, musical works and short stories are required to depict women and girls in a positive manner and/or have lead roles for women actors over forty.

The Columbine Award Competition will also be open to men for the first time, and all films and screenplays, stageplays, radio scripts, TV scripts, musical works and short stories for that contest must reflect non-violent conflict resolution, alternatives to violence or show why a violent resolution to conflict is counter-productive and inhumane. Submitted material may contain violence, but not gratuitous violence.

The Spirit of Moondance Awards category will remain for women only. The films and screenplays, stageplays, radio scripts, TV scripts, and short stories for that category may have men who worked on it, but it must be submitted by either the woman writer, director, cinematographer, editor, and/or producer. Male co-writers are OK. There are no limits or restrictions on content or genre.

NEW! The Dolphin Contest for boys and girls. Young filmmakers are encouraged to submit their short films, documentaries and animation films, in any genre, to Moondance. We wish to motivate and inspire youngsters to freely express themselves and tell their stories from their unique perspective and to film their impressions of the world. Any entrant, age 18 or younger, is welcome.

A note about non-violence in film and The Columbine Award: Moondance is *not* seeking only non-violent works! This is a common misconception. We want to either show alternatives to violent conflict-resolution, or show why and how violent conflict resolution is counter-productive, via our Columbine Awards. All six of the Columbine winners (2000 and 2001) deal with very violent subjects: The Gulf War, apartheid in South Africa, The Troubles in Northern Ireland, World War I, Nazis in post-war Argentina and the Holocaust. Actually, no one, so far, has been able to come up with viable alternatives, but they have shown how violent resolutions do not solve the conflict. We had a large panel discussion and dialogue at Moondance 2001 on this vital subject.

> **“**Less is more. Kill any dialogue that follows, 'I remember' or, 'When I was young.'**”**
>
> —from *Screenwriting 434*
> by Lew Hunter

ADVENTURES IN JUDGING SCREENPLAY ENTRIES

Twenty Ways to Better Your Chances of Winning
by Elizabeth English, Founder and Executive Director,
Moondance International Film Festival

1. Send your submissions in early. Don't wait until the final dead-line date. Your submission can be buried under a pile of hun-dreds or thousands at the bigger festivals and competitions.

2. Two words: Two brads. Brass brads, solid brass brads #6, not those short, wimpy brass-plate brads that let the script fall apart by page sixty. Readers curl the script pages behind what they've read; they leave them overnight, half-read, to read tomorrow. Your script will be roughly handled, often by three or more peo-ple. Make sure it will stay together through all of that!

3. Covers: please use plain cover-stock or card-stock. Print only the script title and author name on the front. Any color is okay, but white, gray or tan are preferred and more professional look-ing. Do not bind your script in a high school plastic binder or one with metal bars inside. Card-stock covers—front and back—are the only acceptable covers.

4. Title Page: Have the first page of your submission be the title page. Print the title, author's name, info on copyright or WGA-registration and the author's contact info: mailing address, phone number and email address. If you change your contact information, let the competition know so they can contact you if you win.

5. Do not write the title or your name on the binding side of the script. That makes the script look old and shopped-around. The competition readers or registration people will do that when they receive the entry.

6. A printed-out copy of the script from your computer looks a lot better than a copy-shop's faded copy. Make sure it's nice and clear and clean, with black ink. It's actually cheaper to print out a computer copy than it is to take it somewhere to be printed, in most cases.

7. Use Courier 12-point font. Nothing else will do.

8. Do not cheat by doing a "loose" script to make your script look like 120-130 pages. Do not do a "tight" script to try to make a too-long script look like 120-130 pages. If you have a 90-page script, that's fine. If you have a 150-page script, you need to do some editing. Check every page of your submission, to make sure it's printed clearly and that the pages are in order and none are missing.

9. Have someone proofread your script for typos, incorrect grammar (except in the dialogue, if that's what you intend), punctuation, spelling, syntax and other errors. (You could offer to pay a dollar for each error found. This will make you really edit in advance to save yourself the expense!) Don't rely only on your spell-check software program. Print out the script and read it in hard copy, and edit as you read. Use a red pen, so you can easily find the edits. Spend the time to correct the errors. Nothing makes an author look more lazy and unprofessional than lots of un-edited errors in your submission.

10. Format. Use the standard script format found in books on the subject and in computer screenwriting programs. Don't customize it. Use correct, standard spacing between elements and in all four of the margins.

11. I love to see the second page of a submission be the logline and mini-synopsis. Production company readers don't usually ask for this or require it, but it makes reading the screenplay a lot easier and more enjoyable. Plus, if your logline is great, it induces the reader to put it at the top of the must-read pile.

12. Don't send in long resumes and lists of credits or info about your other festival wins with your entry forms and submission. It won't help you win. It won't (or shouldn't) influence the readers and judges, because each festival has a different criteria.

13. Entry fees. Attach the check or money order with a paper clip to the front of the entry form. If it's an American competition, make sure the funds are in U.S. dollars. Don't just toss the entry fee into the bottom of the envelope or it may get lost. When sending a money order, write your name on it, so we know whom it's from. When sending a check from someone else, write your name on it, for the same reason.

14. Mailing. Use the simplest packaging possible—one that's easy and quick to open. Don't tape the package together with rolls of duct tape; you're mailing a script, not Kugerrands. Avoid using those envelopes that are full of gray fluffy stuff that gets all over desks and clothes and the floor when the reader has finally managed to slice it open. A script does not need a padded envelope.

15. Postage. Use enough postage to cover the cost of mailing. Most competitions cannot pay the postage due, and your entry will probably be returned to you, unopened.

16. Entry forms and release forms. Fill them out clearly in black ink. Sign them. Print them, rather than using fancy cursive writing in purple or pink ink. Make sure your email address is clear. If you have a mix of zeros (0) and the letter O, make sure they can be read for what they are. Same with the l and 1, or L and lower-case l. They all look the same sometimes, so be clear, if you ever want to hear from the competition again.

17. Remember to enclose the entry form, release form and entry fee with your script in the same envelope.

18. If you want a confirmation that your submission was received, please send (with your submission package) an attached post card with postage. Write on the postcard: name and address, and on the back write the following: We have received your submission (title) on this date.

19. Do bother sending a SASE (self-addressed, stamped envelope) with your submission if the competition says that they will not return any submissions.

20. Make sure your entire submission package is reader-friendly.

MORROW SCREENWRITING FELLOWSHIP

Purpose:	To educate and promote screenwriting in Minnesota. We are looking to reward writers with a clear, original vision and an excellent mastery of craft. Judging criteria is included in the application packet.
Year began:	1997
Categories:	Feature length or Short (12 pages or less).
Sponsor:	Minnesota Screenwriters Workshop
Phone:	(612) 824-9794
Email:	mnsww@mm.com
Website:	mm.com/user/mnsww
Deadline:	Fall
Note:	The Morrow Screenwriting Fellowship is currently being reorganized. Check the Minnesota Screenwriting Workshop website for future details.

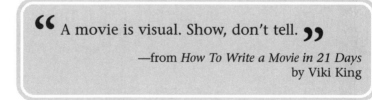

❝ A movie is visual. Show, don't tell. **❞**

—from *How To Write a Movie in 21 Days*
by Viki King

NANTUCKET FILM FESTIVAL
SCREENPLAY COMPETITION

Purpose:	To create an opportunity for unproduced screenwriters to showcase their craft to the industry.
Entry fee:	$40
Year began:	1996
Categories:	Anyone can enter. All subjects, genres are acceptable.
Sponsor:	Nantucket Film Festival
Address:	Nantucket Film Festival Screenplay Competition P.O. Box 688 Prince Street Station New York, NY 10012-0012
Phone:	(212) 708-1278
Fax:	(212) 473-0713
Email:	info@ackfest.org
Website:	www.nantucketfilmfestival.org
Deadline:	March 10
Rules:	Standard format, 90-130 pages. Cannot have won an award from another competition. Not produced, optioned, sold material. Must be copyrighted or registered.
Best Advice:	What appeals to us is original vision. Use proper format. Follow the rules carefully.
Director:	Jonathan Burkhart, Founder/Executive Director; Evan Nagorski, Director
Judges:	Industry professionals.
Cash prizes:	Check with contest.
Non-cash prizes:	Publicity, contacts, readings, awards.

NASHVILLE SCREENWRITERS CONFERENCE
SCREENWRITING COMPETITION

Purpose:	To promote quality material and get it in the hands of producers and agency reps in Los Angeles and New York City.
Entry fee:	$30
Year began:	2000
Categories:	Feature film screenplays
Sponsor:	Nashville Screenwriters Conference and Tennessee Screenwriting Association
Address:	Nashville Screenwriters Conference Screenwriting Competition c/o Tennessee Screenwriting Assoc. P.O. Box 40194 Nashville, TN 37204
Phone:	(615) 316-9448
Email:	free8196@juno.com
Website:	www.tennscreen.com (Entry form, rules, awards, more)
Deadline:	March 31
Rules:	Standard format, 90-130 pages, original material, cannot have been optioned or sold (see website for more).
Best Advice:	Send your strongest stuff and don't be afraid of the genre/content of your story. Have a protagonist pushing the story forward with a goal in mind and by all means have an antagonist keeping your hero from that goal. Don't go over 130 pages. Format it correctly. Show it, don't say it!
Director:	Alan McKenna, TSA VP–Contest Chair
Judges:	First round by Tennessee Screenwriters Association, second round by other industry professionals attending Conference.
Cash prizes:	First place: $1,000; second place: $500; third place: $250.

Non-cash prizes: First place receives a pass and accommodations to the Nashville Screenwriters Conference; Winners submitted to producers and agency representatives, publicity, more.

TIPS

from *Writing Great Characters* by Michael Halpern, Ph.D.

PROTAGONIST'S REWARD
Defeating the literal enemy, or the psychic enemy of self, leads to the reward, which may be a physical prize, the princess, love, or any number of things.

CREATING CHARACTERS
A character's life does not begin at FADE IN or end at FADE OUT. They represent boundaries around a portion of the character's existence.

OPPOSING FORCES
Take a good look at most motion pictures, television, plays, novels, or short stories. In almost every case the stories burst out when an imbalance occurs between characters or between characters and their environment. The imbalance often moves from one extreme to another.

CHARACTER DEVELOPMENT
Character development represents the heart of the writing process.

CREATING THREE-DIMENSIONAL CHARACTERS
A modest command of psychological underpinnings helps develop motivation for our creations. Without that knowledge, protagonists and antagonists remain mere words as two-dimensional as the paper upon which we inscribe them.

NATIONAL SCREENWRITING COMPETITION

Purpose:	To reward screenwriters for outstanding writing.
Entry fee:	$45
Year began:	1999
Categories:	Feature film screenplays
Sponsor:	National Screenwriting Competition
Address:	National Screenwriting Competition 145 Broad St. Matawan, NJ 07747
Phone:	(732) 566-1800
Fax:	(732) 566-7336
Email:	director@skyweb.net
Website:	www.nationalscreenwriting.com (Rules, guidelines, application, FAQ, more)
Deadline:	June 30
Rules:	Submit a completed, signed application form, original material, 90-130 pages, in English. Material cannot be returned. No optioned or sold material at time of submission. Name, address and phone should not appear on the cover, title page or any other page. No substituted or corrected pages accepted. Standard format and brad binding.
Best Advice:	Capture the reader within the first 10-15 pages.
Director:	Seamus O'Fionnghusa
Judges:	Contest director, industry producers, agents, development executives.
Cash prizes:	First place: $2,500; second place: $500; third place: $250 (Judges reserve the right to grant no awards if, in the opinion of the Judges, no entry is of sufficient merit).
Non-cash prizes:	Possible production or development.

NEVADA FILM OFFICE
ANNUAL SCREENPLAY COMPETITION

Purpose:	To promote Nevada writers and statewide locations.
Entry fee:	$15 Nevada resident, $30 non-resident
Year began:	1987
Categories:	Open to all writers. Feature length screenplays.
Sponsor:	Nevada Film Office
Address:	Nevada Film Office 555 E. Washington Ave. #5400 Las Vegas, NV 89134
Phone:	(702) 486-2711 or 877-NEV-FILM
Fax:	(702) 486-2712
Email:	lvnfo@bizopp.state.nv.us
Website:	www.nevadafilm.com (Rules, forms)
Deadline:	Accepted from May 1—June 30
Rules:	Seventy-five percent of locations must be filmable in Nevada. Only top three scripts from any previous Nevada competition are prohibited from entering. No pornography. 90-120 pages, standard industry format. (See website for more.)
Best advice:	If the wrong format is used, they are going to toss it, even if it's the greatest script in the world.
Director:	Jeanne Corcoran, Production Coordinator
Judges:	First round is staff; final round professionals in the industry.
Cash prizes:	No
Non-cash prizes:	Software, certificate, readings, publicity.

WRITE OF WAY

Aspiring Screenwriters Get a Boost from the Nevada Film Office
by Jerry Fink, *Las Vegas Sun*, January 21, 2000

Housewives, DJs, boxing promoters—who knows who tomorrow's crop of rich and famous Hollywood screenwriters will be?

The Nevada Film Office is doing its part to find them, and at the same time attract producers to the state.

Las Vegas producers Dimitri Sotirakis and Kimberlie Chambers of DK Productions are doing their part to find them, which they feel will help sow the seeds that will grow a new Hollywood in the high desert country.

Aspiring writers all over the world are doing their part, submitting their un-produced scripts to the annual Nevada Film Office Screenwriters Competition.

"We've had submissions from as far away as Germany and Japan," said Jeanne Corcoran, Film Office spokeswoman.

The office recently announced the winners of the 1999 competition, the 12th contest sponsored by the office whose job is to encourage those who make films to make them in Nevada.

The top three scripts include *Double Down*, a comedy by Buddy Baron, a DJ in Bossier City, LA; *The Magic Ring*, a fantasy by Henderson Smith, a former health administrator living in Phoenix, AZ; and *One Step Ahead*, an action/road picture by Norwalk, CT, resident Andrew Schub.

Of the top ten scripts, only one came from Las Vegas: *Vegas Rules*, by William S. Reed and Mike Pacitto.

There are a number of rules that must be followed by entrants—the primary one being that 75 percent of the script they submit must be able to be shot in Nevada.

"The scenes can be generic desert, small towns, flat lands, caves, tunnels or the Strip, it doesn't matter as long as 75 percent of them can be shot in the state," Corcoran said.

The top three scripts will be submitted to a group of producers and production companies in Los Angeles for consideration. The remaining seven of the top ten will be given contacts where their scripts have the best chance to be seriously read.

"This is a wonderful opportunity for writers and it is good for the state as well," Charles Geocaris, director of the Film Office, said.

Geocaris came to Las Vegas from Chicago, where he was director of the Chicago Film Office. Chicago began a script-writing competition about five years ago, but it is restricted to Illinois residents.

"We would get 2,700 submissions a year," he said.

Because, relatively speaking, Nevada is so sparsely populated, admissions are accepted from everywhere. About 100 make the first round of judging each year. Many entries are thrown out because they don't follow the basic formatting guidelines, which may be found on the Film Office website at www.nevadafilm.com.

"Ours is the oldest state-sponsored screenplay competition for unsold writers," Corcoran noted. "It is a great opportunity for those who have not sold or optioned a script before."

Winners of the state competition are assured a fair read from interested professionals. In addition to a reading that could launch their career, the top three screenwriters will receive a number of prizes—including professional scriptwriting software—and a luncheon in their honor.

The 1999 winner, Buddy Baron, was a DJ on Las Vegas' KFMS in the mid-90s. He expressed sincere gratitude to the Film Office for giving him his opportunity. "They are a very aggressive little office," he said. *Double Down* is his story about a man who wins a free trip to Las Vegas in a radio contest. The hero looks like a Mafia don and spends his weekend in Vegas running for his life.

Baron, who is a professional comedy writer as well as radio announcer, said he decided to write his script when he had some time on his hands last year. Since then he has written three more scripts.

"The contest is a huge leg up," Baron said. "It's hard enough to get anyone to read a script."

Smith, who formerly lived in Elko but resides temporarily in Phoenix, won second place honors for *The Magic Ring*, her script about the twelve-year-old daughter of a Las Vegas showgirl who finds a magic ring that brings people back from the dead. The girl brings back Marilyn Monroe and Elvis.

"I started writing about a year and a half ago," Smith, 42, said, adding that when she turned 40 she decided to pursue her writing interests in earnest, packing up and moving to Arizona. "I gave it a year," she said.

Las Vegas homemaker Andrea Sweet, 38, was among the top ten screenwriters from the 1998 class of entrants—although she was not among the top three. "The contest is a great way to showcase your writing," she said.

She said that a producer gave her script, called *Sage Sex*, serious consideration, but then decided not to do it. "It wasn't really the genre they were looking for at the time," Sweet said.

She continues to send the script to producers while working on other writing projects and taking care of her seven-year-old son. "I do most of my writing at two or three in the morning, whenever something comes to me," she said. "I try to write something every day."

Sotirakis and Chambers of DK Productions have been working with Las Vegas scriptwriter Mark Zeitoun, who won first place in 1998 for a dramatic script entitled *Strings*. Sotirakis said the script his company is producing is *Help Wanted*, which was written before *Strings*. The earlier script is on hold while Zeitoun is working to get *Strings* produced.

While DK Productions' main focus is on commercials for several casinos and other businesses, Sotirakis has done a number of feature films in the past and wants to do more in the future. He said that the screenwriter's competition is a fertile ground for finding aspiring writers.

"The key in Hollywood is the writing," Sotirakis said. "If you can write, you've got it made."

By promoting scripts based in Nevada, the interest in coming here broadens. "Right now movies are coming here for the background shots," Chambers noted.

Sotirakis and Chambers are confident that it is only a matter of time before Las Vegas takes on the trappings of a Hollywood—it just takes time, patience, lots of money and efforts such as those being made by the Film Office.

"This town needs to stimulate that kind of business growth," Sotirakis said. "We're not a small town anymore. Hollywood is taking a serious look at us."

NEW CENTURY WRITER AWARDS

Purpose:	To provide a new outlet for writers; to recognize and develop quality screenplays, and to connect these writers with industry professionals. (New Century Writer Awards is a not-for-profit, educational organization.)
Entry fee:	$30
Year began:	1998
Categories:	Any genre, all styles.
Sponsor:	New Century Writer Awards
Address:	New Century Writer Awards 32 Alfred St. #B New Haven, CT 06512-3927
Phone:	(203) 469-8824, 888-383-3339
Fax:	(203) 468-0333
Email:	newcenturywriter@yahoo.com
Website:	www.newcenturycinema.org
Deadline:	March 3
Rules:	See website.
Best Advice:	Write a screenplay that resonates in reader's minds. The story should stay with the reader after they put the script down. Think of what stories you remember most and why. Entertain on the surface but let the story run deep with meaning and metaphor. Do not be afraid of emotion, but do not be maudlin. Read a great deal. We want to read character-driven stories for our art house alliances, and high concept stories for our Hollywood studio alliances.
Director:	Jason J. Marchi, Executive Director
Judges:	25-35 first level readers, 10-12 final judges-writers, editors, producers, actors, and others.
Cash prizes:	First place: $5,000; second place: $2,000; third place: $1,000; fourth-tenth place: $250.
Non-cash prizes:	Subscription, publicity, more.
Success story:	Representation, options.

NEW MILLENNIUM CELEBRATIONS
SCREENPLAY CONTEST

Purpose:	To enhance the availability of quality screenplays.
Entry fee:	Early: $25, Standard: $35, Final: $45
Year began:	1998
Categories:	Big Budget, Low Budget, Drama, Short Film and TV Sitcoms
Sponsor:	BDR Productions
Address:	BDR Screenplay Division P.O. Box 3489 Chatsworth, CA 91313-3489
Email:	jennifer@filmmakers.com
Website:	www.filmmakers.com (Guidelines, contests, submitting, more)
Deadlines:	Early: February 29, Standard: March 31, Final: April 28
Rules:	Anyone can enter. More than one script may be submitted. No documentaries. Work must be available for option or purchase. Numbered pages. Do not send additional materials. Copyright your material. Material will not be returned. Font should be Courier 12pt., white 8.5x11 paper, bound with 2-3 brads 1 1/4"-1 1/2" size, covers should be card stock. Include a cover page with only the title and another cover page with your name, title, address, phone number, etc. apart from the script.
	Big Budget: relatively expensive to produce (expansive locations, special effects, elaborate props and costumes, many characters).
	Low Budget: relatively inexpensive to produce (contemporary setting, minimal special effects, props, characters, etc.).
	Drama: story driven.
	Short Film and TV sitcoms: Screenplays 30-50 pages. The sitcom scripts should be original.

Best Advice:	Write a good story! Scripts must conform to industry standards. Avoid directing the script with camera angles. Reduce scene and characters descriptions. We can't say enough about typos and grammar. Please proof read your script before you submit it.
Director:	Jennifer Brooks, FilmMakers.com
Judges:	BDR Productions
Cash prizes:	First place: $2,500; second place: $500; third place: $250; thirty prizes of $100.
Non-cash prizes:	One full scholarship to the Motion Picture Production Program at Victoria Motion Picture School, software, magazine subscriptions, possible option, more.
Success story:	Many being made for television.

> **"**Much of the industry talks in *TV Guide* loglines. These are a good way to test an idea for a spec script.**"**
>
> —from *How To Sell Your Screenplay: The Real Rules of Film and Television Screenwriting* by Carl Sautter

NEW ORLEANS SCREENPLAY COMPETITION

Purpose:	To give novice writers exposure to top executives in the film industry.
Entry fee:	Early: $30, Standard: $40, Final: $50
Year began:	1996
Categories:	All genres accepted.
Address:	New Orleans Screenplay Competition P.O. Box 140 221 Jaguar Blvd. Arabi, LA 70032
Phone:	(504) 276-1780
Email:	gmcgov@acadiacom.net
Deadlines:	Early: before November 1, Standard before January 1, Final: before March 1
Rules:	Do not send original script; screenplays will not be returned. Must be original work. Use industry format, bound with brass brads and cover stock. Do not put your name on the cover. First page should have only the title. Use a separate page for contact information. Judge's decision is final.
Director:	David O'Donnell, Director of Development
Judges:	Industry professionals
Prizes:	Contact contest.

THE NEW YORK INTERNATIONAL
LATINO FILM FESTIVAL

Purpose:	To encourage and support Latino screenwriters,
Entry fee:	See website.
Year began:	2001
Categories:	Feature length screenplays
Sponsor:	MTV Films in 2001
Address:	250 West 26th Street 4th Floor New York, NY 10001
Phone:	(646) 638-1493
Email:	Juanc@nylatinofilm.com
Website:	www.NYLATINOFILM.com
Deadline:	See website.
Rules:	Open to Latino writers with feature length screenplays written in English.
Best Advice:	Read the rules!!! Be on point!
Director:	Juan Caceres
Judges:	Various judges from studio executives to agents.
Cash prizes:	$1,000.
Non-cash prizes:	A 'Roger' award designed by artist James Knowles and a live, staged reading.

NICHOLL FELLOWSHIPS IN SCREENWRITING

Purpose: To assist screenwriters and the art of screenwriting.

Entry fee: $30

Year began: 1988

Categories: Feature length screenplays

Sponsor: Academy Foundation

Address: Nicholl Fellowships In Screenwriting
                     Academy Foundation
                     8949 Wilshire Blvd.
                     Beverly Hills, CA 90211-1972

Phone: (310) 247-3000

Email: nicholl@oscars.org

Website: www.oscars.org/nicholl.
                     (Rules, FAQ, history, more)

Deadline: May 1

Rules: No applicant may have earned more than $5,000
                     for screenwriting. 100-130 pages, standard industry
                     format, in English (see website for more).

Best Advice: Write a really good screenplay, follow the rules,
                     get lucky.

Director: Greg Beal, Program Coordinator

Judges: Academy Foundation

Cash prizes: Up to five $25,000 fellowships.

Non-cash prizes: Publicity, industry contacts.

Success story: Representation, options.

OFF THE PAGE TORONTO SCREENPLAY READINGS

Purpose:	To give writers audience feedback and promote script to industry buyers.
Entry fee:	$35 (Canadian or U.S.)
Year began:	2000
Categories:	All genres accepted.
Sponsor:	Off the Page
Address:	238 Davenport Rd. # 415 Toronto, Ontario, M5R 1J6, Canada
Phone:	(416) 944-1912
Email:	mitch@offthepage.org
Website:	www.offthepage.org
Deadline:	Quarterly, 15th of March, June, September and December
Rules:	1) Script must be available. 2) The writer(s) must own rights. 3) Resubmissions are allowed. 4) Minimum 87, maximum 120 pages.
Best Advice:	"Small," indie-style scripts preferred. Take the "live reading" format into account—long action sequences don't play as well as meaty dialogue.
Director:	Mitch Moldofsky
Judges:	Mitch Moldofsky
Non-cash prizes:	Screenplay reading in cafe setting, written audience feedback, videotape of reading, line edit and consultation on script, promotion on website.

DO IT YOURSELF!

by Off The Page Toronto Screenplay Readings

Any writer can benefit from hearing his or her script read aloud by actors, and it's not as difficult to organize as it might seem. Here is a step-by-step guide:

- Find actors in your area, or write a short notice such as "ACTORS NEEDED FOR SCREENPLAY READINGS."
- Rent a space or use your living room; provide food.
- Cast only as many as four to seven parts for the reading.
- Do not read the stage directions yourself, let one of the actors.
- Allow thirty minutes or so for feedback at the end of the reading.
- Wait at least 24 hours before you rewrite!

OHIO INDEPENDENT SCREENPLAY AWARDS

Entry fee: $40/early by May 15; $60 late by June 1

Year began: 1997

Categories: Best Screenplay and Best Northcoast Screenplay
                    (most of the action set in Northern Ohio).

Sponsor: Ohio Independent Film Festival

Address: 1392 West 65th Street
                    Cleveland, Ohio 44102

Phone: (216) 781-1755

Fax: (216) 651-7317

Email: OhioIndieFilmFest@juno.com

Website: www.ohiofilms.com

Deadline: Early: postmarked by May 15;
                    Late: postmarked by June 1

Rules: Submit two copies of script along with entry fee
                    and entry form.

Best Advice: Check your spelling and grammar.

Director: Bernadette Gillota and Annetta Marion

Judges: Varies

Cash prizes: $1,000 cash to each winner.

Non-cash prizes: Unstaged reading at the festival and subscription to
                    Scr(i)pt magazine, submission to a literary agent.

Success story: One winner from the 2000 contest is currently writ-
                    ing a pilot in Los Angeles, got the job directly from
                    her contacts through the Ohio Independent
                    Screenplay Awards.

THE ONE IN TEN SCREENPLAY COMPETITION

Purpose:	To positively portray gays and lesbians in film.
Entry fee:	$40
Year began:	1997
Categories:	General. At least one of the primary characters in the screenplay should be gay or lesbian, and gay and lesbian characters must be portrayed positively. Gay and Lesbian writers are encouraged to enter!
Sponsor:	Cherub Productions
Address:	One In Ten Screenplay Competition P.O. Box 540 Boulder, CO 80306
Phone:	(303) 629-3072
Fax:	(801) 729-6473
Email:	cherubfilm@aol.com
Website:	www.screenplaycontests.com
Deadline:	September 1
Rules:	Screenplays must not have been previously optioned, produced or purchased prior to September 1, 2001. Screenplays must be original work of applicant(s). Winning screenplay submissions written by two or more writers require all awards to be divided equally among the writers. Screenplays must be in English. Multiple submissions are accepted but each submission requires a separate entry form and separate fee. Screenplays must be between 90-125 pages. Cherub Productions is not responsible for screenplays lost, stolen, or lost in shipping. Judges decisions are final. Each submission must be accompanied by submission form/fee. Screenplays must contain at least one gay or lesbian primary character. Screenplays must portray gay and lesbian characters positively. Entry must be postmarked by September 1, 2001.

Submissions must be in standard motion picture script format. Submissions must be accompanied by entry form. Only the title should appear on the script title page. Author(s) name(s) should not appear anywhere on the script. Each submission must include a synopsis of four sentences or less. Submissions will not be returned. See website for more details.

Best Advice: Get your script out there; enter contests, develop industry relationships, get an agent, be persistent. "Many individuals in Hollywood have become famous simply because they didn't quit when they should have."

Director: David Jensen

Judges: Industry professionals

Cash prizes: First place: $500 cash prize and submission to a major film studio and literary agent; second place: $250 cash prize and submission to a major film studio; third place: $100 cash prize and screenplay software.

Non-cash prizes: See website.

Success story: We're a fairly new contest. Our scripts are being read by top studio executives.

OPEN DOOR CONTEST

Purpose:	To discover, promote and recognize a talented new screenwriter.
Entry fee:	$40
Category:	No pornography. All other genres accepted.
Sponsor:	*Scr(i)pt* magazine (A progressive and legitimate agency, management company, or production company seeking quality material co-sponsors each contest.)
Address:	Open Door Contest c/o *Scr(i)pt* magazine 5638 Sweet Air Rd. Baldwin, MD 21013
Phone:	(410) 592-3466
Fax:	(410) 592-8062
Website:	www.scriptmag.com (Application, release, rules, fee, deadline, format, judging criteria, FAQs, do's and don'ts [see following], more)
Deadlines:	Quarterly (check with contest).
Rules:	Do not send original script; material will not be returned. Do not put your name anywhere on the script. Industry format. Recommend copyright or registration of script. Must own the script. Writer cannot have received consideration of any kind for screenwriting work over a $5,000 value. Original work of author. No adaptations. Written in English. Must be at least 18 years old. No limit to number of entries per author. Include SASE for notification. Length 90-130 pages, bound with brads, using 12 point Courier font. Do not include additional materials. Please do not send any special packaging gimmicks.
Best Advice:	Please read and adhere to the contest rules carefully. It is very important that you submit your script as if you were submitting it to an actual production company.
Director:	Diane Baylin, Editor

Judges:	Professional industry readers will read up to at least page 30 of each script.
Cash prizes:	First place: $3,000.
Non-cash prizes:	Film festival trip, industry contacts, notes, publicity.

DO'S AND DON'TS

of Entering Your Script in the Open Door Contest, sponsored by *Scr(i)pt* magazine

DON'T:
- Write your name anywhere on the script.
- Include cast lists, resumes, musical scores, illustrations, etc.
- Use CUT TO:
- Use too many parentheticals.
- Write CONTINUED on every page.
- Use work/ideas/stories/characters which are under copywrite by someone else.
- Send revisions.
- Forget to sign a release form.
- Contact the sponsors of the contest directly. If you have questions, use email.
- Use binders or non-industry standard bindings.

DO:
- Use industry standard format.
- Bind your script securely using brass brads or Chicago screws.
- Spell and grammar check, and proofread very carefully.
- Get to the point of your story quickly.
- Be descriptive rather than specific when giving camera directions.
- Keep the pace moving throughout your story.
- Write visually—if you can't see it on the screen, don't write it.

ORANGE SCREENWRITING PRIZE

Purpose:
To help support and sustain the current enthusiasm for British film. Its investment is aimed at providing long-term financial and practical support for the wealth of as yet undiscovered talent.

Entry fee:
£30 plus British value added tax

Address:
The Orange Prize for Screenwriting
PO Box 2721
London, England W1A 5BJ

Website:
www.pathe.com.uk/screenwriting/1.html

Rules:
Entrants must be British citizens or residents in the UK. Your script should be for an entertaining contemporary feature film set in Britain, with wide audience appeal. The script should fall within one of three popular genres: thriller, comedy or love story. Even if you think that your script has elements of all three, you should decide which category is the most appropriate for your script.

Best Advice:
Typewritten on A4 paper, maximum of 120 pages, standard screenplay format.

Cash prizes:
Three writers will be awarded £10,000. One screenplay will be produced.

OSCAR MOORE PRIZE

Purpose:	European scriptwriting prize launched in memory of film journalist Oscar Moore.
Address:	Oscar Moore Foundation 33-39 Bowling Green Lane London EC1R 0DA
Phone:	0171 5058 112
Fax:	0171 5058 116
Website:	www.lsw.org.uk/hotnews.htm (Check the website, or write to the Foundation for more information.)
Rules:	Screenwriter must be a European National. Screenplay must be a contemporary European thriller, feature length, no more than 120 pages, in English.
Cash prizes:	£10,000.

> **"**The most important facet of story craft is structure. It is no coincidence, and also perfectly predictable, that by the end of the middle, virtually every screenplay runs headlong into a formidable barrier. The baseball community addresses this problem with a well-respected convention: the seventh-inning stretch. This is where all appears lost—The Big Gloom—approximately 80 minutes into the film.**"**
>
> —from *Screenwriting: The Art, Craft and Business of Film and Television*
> by Richard Walter

PACIFIC NORTHWEST WRITERS CONFERENCE LITERARY CONTEST

Purpose:

To help writers maximize their efforts, while honoring and recognizing the best of new writing, and to provide brief but relevant evaluations for all entries.

Entry fee:

PNWC members $25, non-members $35

Year began:

1956

Categories:

Open to anyone. Screenplay or teleplay.

Sponsor:

Pacific Northwest Writers Association (PNWA)

Address:

PNWA Literary Contest
2608 3rd Ave. #B
Seattle, WA 98121

Phone:

(206) 728-8570

Email:

contest@pnwa.org

Website:

www.pnwa.org.

Deadline:

February 15 (see website).

Rules:

Include a synopsis, not to exceed five double-spaced pages. Submit full script. (See website for more.)

Best Advice:

Follow the rules. Use professional format. Treat it like a business.

Judges:

PNWA

Cash prizes:

Over $8,000 in cash prizes distributed in eight categories.

Non-cash prizes: Publicity.

THE PAGE ONE CONTEST

Purpose:	To draw attention to the importance of the first page of a screenplay.
Entry fee:	$20
Year began:	1998
Categories:	All genres accepted.
Sponsor:	The Screenwriters Group
Address:	Page One Screenwriting contest 1803 W. Bryon Chicago, IL 60613
Phone:	(773) 665-8500
Fax:	(773) 665-9475
Email:	Dan@screenwritersgroup.com
Website:	www.AnatomyofaScreenplay.com
Deadline:	December 31 of each year.
Rules:	Submit one page, standard screenplay format. Must begin with FADE IN. Open to everyone. No restrictions.
Best Advice:	Make every word count. Knock us out with your imagery, text, subtext and character.
Director:	Dan Decker
Judges:	Staff instructors at Screenwriters Group.
Non-cash prizes:	Winning entry is printed as written in a full page ad in a national trade magazine.
Success story:	Previous winners have appeared in the *Hollywood Reporter* and *Scr(i)pt* magazine.

THE WINNING SCRIPT

Page One Screenwriting Contest 1999

The Screenwriter's Group, a screenplay development company, is proud to present the winner of its unique, one-page screenwriting competition for 1999: Frank Leimbeck . . .

```
FADE IN

INT. BEDROOM - NIGHT

The room is decorated with science
charts, books, and a poster of Einstein.

STEVEN STUART, 11, wearing goggles, works
on a homemade device constructed of a
cardboard box, colored wires, batteries
and computer components.

MOTHER'S VOICE
          It's time for bed, Steven.

STEVEN
          I want everything to go
          perfect for the science fair.

His door opens and MOTHER, smiling but
concerned, looks in.

MOTHER
          Did you take your medicine?

Steven continues to work and nods.

MOTHER (cont'd)
          I love you.

STEVEN
          Love you too.
```

She closes the door. Steven sits in the box and types on a small computer. With a deep breath, he presses a button.

Lights flash. Beeps sound. The desk, bed, and walls slowly melt as Steven looks around in wonder.

STEVEN
          Yes.

A blinding flash of light fills the room.

INT. CAVE - NIGHT

A large DRAGON SNORTS and PUFFS FIRE. Steven, cardboard box and all, material- izes before the dragon.

It snorts and Steven screams. The box catches fire. Steven rolls out. The drag- on flees.

OTTO, 13, dressed in armor, carrying a sword, rushes after the Dragon but stops.

THE PEOPLE'S PILOT

Purpose: To enable new writers to sell a television series.

Entry fee: $40

Year began: 2000

Categories: Open to all TV genres.

Sponsor: TV Writer.com and Brody Productions

Address: Cloud Creek Ranch
422 West Carlisle Road
Westlake Village, CA 91361

Fax: (805) 495-3659

Email: lbrody@tvwriter.com

Website: http://www.tvwriter.com

Deadline: June 1 and December 1 every year.

Rules: Not a teleplay contest, but an idea contest. Please submit a five-page presentation of your series, including its general premise, continuing characters and potential storylines.

Best Advice: Be fresh, new—and brief!

Director: Larry Brody

Judges: Larry Brody, Mark Lichtman, Peggy Patrick

Cash prizes: One-year option at WGA minimum for first place winner, offered by Brody Productions.

Non-cash prizes: Packaging representation for the series for first, second and third place winners by the Shapiro-Lichtman Agency.

Success story: The network and cable channel response to winners and finalists has been excellent, with many networks "unofficially" working with the material.

PRAXIS CENTRE FOR SCREENWRITERS
SCREENPLAY COMPETITION

Purpose:	Looking for independent dramatic scripts with artistic merit, preferably films that can be produced in Canada.
Entry fee:	$65
Year began:	1986
Categories:	Feature film screenplays. All genres. (Open only to Canadian citizens or Landed Immigrants.)
Sponsor:	Praxis Centre for Screenwriters
Address:	Praxis Film Development Workshop The Mews #300-12 Water St. Vancouver, British Columbia, Canada V6B 1A5
Phone:	(604) 682-3100
Fax:	(604) 682-7909
Email:	praxis@sfu.ca
Website:	www.praxisfilm.com
Deadline:	June 30, October 30
Rules:	Send three properly bound copies, entry fee, application form, resume and a one-page synopsis.
Best advice:	Standard industry format and bound with brads. Proofread. Don't use a cutesy title. If you've seen it already, don't write it. Write something you care about enough to write ten or more drafts of.
Director:	Patricia Gruben
Judges:	Screenwriters, story editors, producers.
Non-cash prizes:	Three to six scripts are chosen for workshop participation.
Success story:	Features and television shows have been produced from alumni.

PRODUCE ME 2002

Purpose:	Production
Entry fee:	$25
Year began:	2000
Categories:	Budget for $1-3 million, all genres accepted.
Sponsor:	Produce Me 2002
Address:	Produce Me 2002 P.O. Box 381 I.T., NY 11752
Phone:	(646) 435-1660
Fax:	(631) 224-8813
Email:	info@produceme2002.com
Website:	www.produceme2002.com
Deadline:	January 9 (see website for future contests)
Rules:	Writer submission codes by state must be included on all submitted materials (see website for codes). Material must be registered. In English and in industry format. Budget for $1-3 million. No pornography.
Best Advice:	Follow the rules. Double check your entry. Adhere to industry format. Submit material that can be produced for under $3 million. That means no big car chases, bombs, guns, etc. No *T-2* or *Die Hard* action scripts because they can't be done for $1-3 million. Write a great story and all mistakes will be forgiven.
Director:	Paige Dillon, Moderator
Judges:	Produce Me 2002 representatives. All entries receive coverage and script notes.
Prizes:	Winner will be produced and released.

PROJECT GREENLIGHT

Purpose:	The winner is eligible to direct their screenplay as a feature film, and the production will be made into a "Making Of . . . " documentary. The documentary will focus on the adventures of a first-time writer/director.
Entry fee:	None
Year began:	2000
Categories:	Live-action feature film
Sponsors:	Ben Affleck, Matt Damon, Chris Moore, Miramax Films and HBO.
Website:	www.projectgreenlight.com (Participant polls, how to participate, calendar, official rules, FAQs)
Deadlines:	Contact contest for this year's deadline.
Rules:	Submit in electronic format only via website. Hardcopy submissions will not be accepted, no exceptions. Written in English, between 90-130 pages, industry format. Work must be previously unproduced. No adaptations. Registered with both the U.S. Copyright Office and WGA.
Best advice:	Do your best so we have some great movies to choose from.
Judges:	Project Greenlight representatives and you! (See website for details on how to be a reviewer.)
Prizes:	Produced as a feature film, and featured as a documentary. Pete Jones, a former insurance salesman, bested more than 7,000 entries and received a $1 million budget from Miramax to make *Stolen Summer*, a drama. (Second place, *Speakeasy*, was also awarded a total of $1 million.) All of the screenplays in the Project Greenlight contest, including the Top 250, Top 30, Top 10 and Top Three, as well as the Top Ten Scenes, can be seen on the Internet at the Project Greenlight website.

LETTER FROM CHRIS MOORE

Greetings potential Filmmakers!

We are thrilled that you have decided to experience the filmmakers process with us from the inside. My name is Chris Moore, and I have had the great opportunity to be a movie producer for the past five years. I have also had the pleasure of working with Matt Damon and Ben Affleck for the past five years. When we made *Good Will Hunting*, we were a lot like you might be right now. We had little experience and only a few industry relationships, but we had what we thought was a great script with two talented actors attached to it. After Castle Rock and Miramax picked us out of the large pool of aspiring filmmakers, it turned out we were right. We fully believed in our project, and this level of belief is what we are asking from you.

It is so hard to get into Hollywood—and so hard to get a movie made even if you *are* in Hollywood—that Matt, Ben and I (along with Miramax and HBO) decided to build a way for you, the struggling screenwriters and filmmakers, to help pick an underdog with us every year. We will make that movie together and help keep new voices coming to Hollywood. That is the purpose of Greenlight.

Matt, Ben and I wish you all luck and inspiration. We want you all to do your best work so we have some great movies to choose from.

PROVIDENCE FILM FOUNDATION
SCREENWRITING COMPETITION

Purpose:	To recognize and reward screenwriters of exceptional talent and vision.
Entry fee:	$35
Categories:	Cannot have sold or optioned a screenplay for more than $1,000.
Sponsor:	Providence Film Foundation, Providence Film Commission, Mayor's Office
Address:	Providence Film Foundation Screenwriting Competition P.O. Box 6705 Providence, RI 02940-6705
Website:	www.providenceri.com/film
Deadline:	May 3
Rules:	Written in English, original work, must not have been sold, optioned, produced. (Contact contest for more.)
Director:	Tom Dooley
Judges:	Industry professionals
Cash prizes:	First place: $2,500; second place: $500; third place: $250.
Non-cash prizes:	Round trip travel, lodging, and tuition to New England Screenwriters Conference, staged reading.

QUANTUM QUEST

Purpose:	To discover and promote original feature and MOW scripts from aspiring writers.
Entry fee:	$45
Year began:	1998
Categories:	Feature films, Movies of the Week
Sponsor:	Quantum United Enterprises
Address:	Quantum United Enterprises 23679 Calabasas Rd. #502 Calabasas, CA 91302
Email:	quequest@flash.net
Deadline:	September 1
Rules:	No produced, sold or optioned material. Finalists in other contests two years prior to this contest are not eligible. Include application and synopsis form. Standard industry format. Material will not be returned. (See website for more details.)
Judges:	Quantum United Enterprises
Cash prizes:	First place: $1,500; second place: $750; third place: $300; fourth place: $100.
Non-cash prizes:	Possible representation, contacts, publicity.

RED INKWORKS SCREENWRITERS CONTEST

Purpose: To create an opportunity for you to present your
              best material to two North American film produc-
              tion companies for the sole purpose of enhancing
              the quality of what appears on the screen.

Entry fee: $35

Year began: 1999

Categories: Open to all, but sponsoring companies favor
              family-oriented, broad-based scripts.

Sponsor: Voyageur Film Capital Corporation/KPE Productions

Address: T. Shaw
              312-125 W. 18th St.
              North Vancouver, BC V7M 1W5

Phone: (604) 984-8372

Email: imyles@direct.ca

Website: www.redinkworks.com

Deadline: May 1

Rules: Copyright or register your script. Industry format.
              Original work, feature length, not optioned, pro-
              duced or already sold. Title page should include
              author name, address, phone number and email.
              Title must appear on the bound edge of the script.
              Three-hole punched, bound with brads. Material
              will not be returned.

Best Advice: Write quality material, with budget-awareness and
              tight writing.

Director: Larry Myles

Judges: Red Inkworks and affiliate companies

Non-cash prizes: Read by professional representatives of high profile,
              award-winning production companies, reading.

ROUGHCUT.COM'S SCREENPLAY CHALLENGE

Purpose:	To allow aspiring screenwriters to collaborate online with professional screenwriters through a ten week round-robin contest.
Entry fee:	None
Year began:	2000
Categories:	Open to all U.S. residents except Florida; must be thirteen years and older. (See website for longer list of those not eligible to participate.)
Sponsor:	Turner Network Television, A Time Warner Company.
Address:	Rough Cut Screenplay Challenge 1050 Techwood Dr. NW Atlanta, GA 30318
Email:	screenplay@roughcut.com
Website:	www.roughcut.com
Deadline:	January 29
Rules:	Entries are considered only for the week they are received. All entries become the property of the Sponsors and will not be returned. (See website for more details.)
Director:	Chris Brandon
Judges:	Professionals in the industry judge based on 25 percent character development, 25 percent plot progression, 25 percent dialogue, 25 percent creativity.
Cash prizes:	$100 weekly (one grand prize winner after eight weeks).
Non-cash prizes:	Laptop computer, certificate, publicity. (See website for approximate market values of prizes.)

SAMUEL GOLDWYN WRITING AWARDS

Purpose:	To support student screenwriters at the University of California (any campus).
Entry fee:	None
Year began:	1956
Categories:	Must be enrolled as a graduate or undergraduate student at the University of California.
Sponsor:	School of Theatre Film and Television/UCLA
Address:	Awards Coordinator School of Theatre Film and Television/UCLA 103 E. Melnitz Los Angeles, CA 90024
Phone:	(310) 206-8441
Fax:	(310) 825-3383
Deadline:	Scripts accepted from March 30 to May 31
Rules:	Open to graduate and undergraduate students of the University of California. Only full-length dramatic writing in proper script format-screenplay or one-hour teleplay. Nothing optioned, produced or sold. Previous submissions are not eligible. Material will not be returned.
Best Advice:	Meticulous care should be taken before submitting. Avoid typos.
Director:	Catherine Hernandez, Awards Coordinator
Judges:	School of Theatre Film and Television/UCLA
Cash prizes:	First place: $10,000; second place: $5,000; third place: $3,000; honorable mention: $2,000 and $1,000.
Non-cash prizes:	Industry contacts, publicity.

SCREEN TEENS

Entry fee:	$15 first entry, $10 each additional entry.
Sponsor:	Final Draft Software
Address:	On Cue Productions Screenwriting competition P.O. Box 535 Yreka, CA 96097
Email:	screenteens@hotmail.com
Website:	http://fade.to/screenteens
Deadline:	There are four contests per year.
Rules:	Must be under age 21. All material containing any of the following will be disqualified: graphic violence, profanity, sexual content, references to drugs and/or illegal substances. If you want your material returned, include a SASE with your submission. Always keep a copy of your work. On Cue Productions is not responsible for material lost in the mail. All deadline dates are final. No late entries, they will be returned with SASE or destroyed. You are responsible for protecting your work by copyright or registration.
Best Advice:	Go for it.
Director:	Leigh Sullivan
Judges:	On Cue Productions staff of young writers
Cash prizes:	$75, $25—first three scripts will be produced on digital video by On Cue Productions.

SCREENPLAYOFF

Purpose:	To offer screenwriters an original format in which they can follow their scripts through the judging process. Writers can track their title through competition brackets on the website.
Entry fee:	$50
Year began:	2000
Categories:	Feature length screenplays, all genres accepted.
Sponsor:	Screenplayoff
Address:	Screenplayoff P.O. Box 49370 Austin, TX 78765
Phone:	(512) 589-6480
Email:	playoff@jump.net
Website:	www.screenplayoff.com (Details, nominations, brackets, Q and A, judges, entry form)
Deadline:	January 15
Rules:	When you enter, you can find your title listed on the website and track it from there. The goal is to have your script chosen as one of sixty-four scripts that will be placed in the brackets. Scripts are bracketed (read) in a one-on-one competition. When your script defeats six other scripts head-to-head, you are a champion. Scripts must be seventy-five pages or more. Follow the website rules and fill out the synopsis section.
Best Advice:	Write a script that will appeal to all kinds of people. You've go to get through at least seven judges to win the tournament. It's impossible to please everyone with story content, but professional writing makes readers smile.
Director:	Tad Cobb
Judges:	Professionals in the industry (writers, directors, producers, story analysts, etc.).

Cash prizes: First place: $5,000; second place: $1,000;
                       semifinalists: $500 each.

Non-cash prizes: Publicity, industry contacts.

TIPS

from *Elements of Style for Screenwriters* by Paul Argentini

BINDING
Some script readers like to take out the fasteners and read the script with loose pages; they can't do this if you have made them tamper-proof. Do not put tape over the ends of the fasteners; do not bend the ends of the fasteners.

CAMERA ANGLES
Camera angles and directions are not necessary in a selling script. If your vision calls for a specific view and a particular camera angle, then find another way to write it. For example, do not write, " LONG SHOT on a flock of crows." A better way is to write, "In the far distance, we SEE a flock of crows."

CUT TO:
Use it sparingly and with discretion, but use it if you must, particularly when there is a dramatic shift in locale.

NARRATIVE
Break long descriptions into three, four, or five sentence paragraphs. Really effective, fast moving action can be achieved by a series of one-sentence descriptions.

CHARACTER NAMES
When a character is introduced for the first time, the CHARACTER NAME is typed in capital letters. Use the same name throughout the script. A character name is never left hanging alone at the bottom of the page.

FADE IN/FADE OUT
The trend is not to begin with FADE IN: Just begin.

The *"FIVE-AND-DIME TREATMENT"*
A simplified method of judging a screenplay by looking at the first five pages and the last ten pages.

SCRIPT LENGTH
One page of screenplay is roughly equal to one minute of screen time. A full-length screenplay runs around 120 pages, although acceptable length can be anywhere from 90 to 130 pages.

(MORE)
is used when a character's speech is interrupted by the end of the page and is continued onto the next page.

MUSIC
is trendy and may not be in vogue by the time your movie is made. Use specific songs only when necessary.

PARENTHETICALS
Anything longer than two lines should be written as direction before or after the character's dialogue ... good writing dictates the mood of the action.

SASE
The acronym for "self-addressed, stamped envelope." Include one if you want your script back.

SCRIPT SPECIFICATIONS
- Use white paper.
- Use 20-lb paper stock.
- Use the standard paper size of 8 1/2" x 11."
- Use a letter-quality printer. Don't use a fancy font. The standard Courier 12 point is generally accepted.
- Don't justify the right-hand margin.
- Send your script through spellcheck.

SENDING OUT SCRIPTS
Do not send a script by registered mail. If you want to know if your script has been received, enclose a self-addressed, stamped postcard and ask the story editor to drop the postcard in the mail.

SCREENWRITING IN THE SUN

Purpose: To connect writers to industry contacts.

Entry fee: Check website.

Category: Feature film

Sponsor: Fort Lauderdale International Film Festival,
                    Scr(i)pt magazine

Address: Open Door Contests
                    5638 Sweet Air Rd
                    Baldwin, MD 21013

Website: www.scriptmag.com

Deadline: See website.

Rules: See website.

Judges: Industry professionals.

Cash prizes: $5,000.

Non-cash prizes: Publicity, festival, more.

> **"**Don't number scenes, use 'continued,' capitalize sound effects, write camera directions, or include a credit sequence.**"**
>
> —from *Writing Screenplays That Sell*
> by Michael Hauge

SCREENWRITING SHOWCASE AWARDS

Purpose: To reward and connect writers to the industry, while providing the tools writers need to succeed.

Entry fee: Early: $25, Final: $30. (You may submit up to three screenplays. Submit 1: $25/$30, submit 2 $45/$50, submit 3 $55/$60.)

Year began: 1995

Categories: Any writer, any genre.

Sponsor: Screenwriting Showcase Awards, Screenwriters Utopia

Address: Screenwriting Showcase Awards
                    attn: Christopher Wehner
                    1511 Lowell Ln.
                    Grand Junction, CO 81506

Phone: (888) 522-6864

Fax: (801) 327-1629

Email: info@screenwritingawards.com

Website: www.screenwritingawards.com
                    (Judges, deadlines, fees, submissions, prizes, more)

Deadlines: October 1

Rules: Not optioned, produced or sold. No more than 90-135 pages; bound by two brass brads. Previous winners are not eligible. (See website for more.)

Best Advice: Write the best script you can. Use standard professional format, bound with brass brads. Present a professional script.

Director: Christopher Wehner

Judges: Working industry professionals (script consultants, writers, industry authors, and contest director).

Cash prizes: First place: $750, second place: $250, special mention $100.

Non-cash prizes: Publicity, industry contacts, industry magazine subscription, software, more.

Success story: Options, assignments.

SCRIPTAPALOOZA, INC. AND SCREENPLAY.COM'S SCREENWRITING COMPETITION

Purpose: To discover talented writers, promote them for a
                   year and create opportunities.

Entry fee: $40-$50

Year began: 1998

Categories: Feature length screenplays, all genres accepted.

Address: 7775 Sunset Blvd. PMB #200
                   Hollywood, CA 90046

Fax: (323) 656-7260

Email: info@scriptapalooza.com

Website: www.scriptapalooza.com

Deadline: Final deadline: April 15 each year.

Rules: Visit website for details.

Best Advice: Rewrite, rewrite, rewrite.

Director: Mark Andrushko, Kelli Bennett, Genevieve Cibor

Judges: Mark Andrushko, Kelli Bennett, Genevieve Cibor

Cash prizes: First place: $25,000; second place: $3,000;
                   third place $2,000 (figures from 2000).

Non-cash prizes: Screenplay.com software to winners, runners-up
                   and finalists.

Success story: Andrea Bailey, a 1999 2nd Place Winner, wrote
                   Falling over Venus which was picked up by Marc Platt
                   Productions, to be set up at Universal, with Mary
                   Stuart Masterson attached to direct. Jamie Wilson,
                   runner-up, wrote *Size Matters* which was optioned
                   by Palooza Pictures. Jamie's script also led to a devel-
                   opment deal with Klasky Csupo Productions.

                   TV Writing Competition: Barbara Schwartz, a final-
                   ist, in the November 1999 television writing com-
                   petition. Her spec script of *Dharma and Greg* led to
                   a development deal with Klasky Csupo Productions.
                   She is now also freelancing for them, writing a
                   Rugrats episode and working on *As Told by Ginger.*

SCRIPTIC GREENLIGHT INTERNATIONAL SCRIPTWRITING COMPETITION

Purpose:	To assist amateur screenwriters who have written scripts or treatments that make a valuable contribution to the arts and culture.
Entry fee:	$35-$95 (Canadian), depending on category.
Year began:	1998
Categories:	Any genre. Original Theatrical, Original Short, Theatrical Adaptation, Short Adaptation, PSA, Treatment
Sponsor:	International Youth Film Festival
Address:	Scriptic Greenlight International Scriptwriting Competition Suite 103-1700 West 75th Ave. Vancouver, BC V6P 6G2
Fax:	(604) 267-3728
Email:	info@greenlightfilm.com
Website:	www.greenlightfilm.org
Deadline:	October 29
Rules:	In English, not optioned, not produced, not sold.
Best Advice:	Judges are looking for: proper formatting, character development, story and content, structure.
Director:	Steve Jones
Judges:	Industry professionals
Cash prizes:	$500-$5,000 depending on category.
Non-cash prizes:	Publicity.

SCRIPTVILLE SCREENWRITING COMPETITION

Purpose:	To help get the unproduced writer through the well-guarded gates of Hollywood.
Entry fee:	Early: $85, Final: $95
Year began:	2000
Categories:	Open to all writers, all genres accepted.
Sponsor:	An alliance of professional Hollywood Script Analysts.
Address:	Scriptville Screenwriting Competition 12439 Magnolia Blvd. #166 N. Hollywood, CA 91607
Phone:	(818) 380-1236
Email:	info@scriptville.com
Website:	www.scriptville.com (Story notes vs. coverage, rules/fees, application, release form)
Deadline:	June 15 (extended)
Rules:	English only. No longer than 139 pages. Must be registered with the WGA or copyrighted. (See website for more.)
Best Advice:	This is highly competitive business, so the craft had better be terrific and/or the story the most original anyone has seen in a long time.
Director:	Dee Hill, Coordinator
Judges:	Professional script analysts
Cash prizes:	$500.
Non-cash prizes:	Winner receives a script consultation from concept to polish; every entrant receives professional story notes.

SCRIPTWRITERS NETWORK, CARL SAUTTER
MEMORIAL SCRIPTWRITING COMPETITION

Purpose:	A support group for people pursuing a scriptwriting career. Designed to help emerging screenwriters gain access to the entertainment industry.
Entry fee:	$30
Year began:	1992
Categories:	Features, MOWs, one-hour and half-hour TV
Sponsor:	Scriptwriters Network (a non-profit organization)
Address:	Scriptwriters Network Carl Sautter Scriptwriting Competition 11684 Ventura Blvd. #508, Studio City, CA 91604
Phone:	(213) 848-9477
Email:	scriptwritersnetwork@artnet.com
Website:	www.scriptwritersnetwork.com (Phases, prizes, forms, instructions, timeline)
Deadline:	May 10
Rules:	Open to Scriptwriters Network members only (you may join when you enter). Script must not have been optioned, sold or produced. No limit on number of entries per person. (See website for more rules.)
Best Advice:	Make sure your script is in proper format. The first 30 pages must grab the reader. In the finals, industry judges look for really good writing and strong storytelling, plus ideas that are fresh and innovative.
Director:	Bill Lundy, Coordinator
Judges:	Industry professionals (see website for judging phases).
Non-cash prizes:	Guaranteed reads by producers, agents, development execs, show runners and other industry professionals; conference, award, books, gift certificates, movie passes, subscriptions, software.
Success story:	Agents, development deals, staff writing jobs.

SERIES SEARCH WRITING CONTEST

Purpose:	1) To locate promising series concepts for potential development for broadcast on an in-house webcast station launching in 2004. 2) To locate near-professional writers to bring to Halifax for a one-year fellowship. The writers will work with teams of third year animation students through their Production Management course to develop a series concept through all development stages up to pre-production. The best of these projects will be added to the webstation programming line-up. Writers may be offered full-time work with Animatrix Productions after the Fellowship is complete.
Entry fee:	$25 (U.S.)
Year began:	2001
Categories:	TV-style series in three age categories: 8-13, 14-17, 18+. We will also be adding two new categories for 2002: Feature film in a special effects genre (sci-fi, action, horror, fantasy) and half hour animated holiday specials.
Sponsor:	Animatrix Productions
Address:	Box 116 1469 Brenton Street Halifax, NS B3J-3W7
Fax:	(902) 484-7691
Email:	Contestquestions@animatrix.ns.ca
Website:	http://www.animatrix.ns.ca
Deadline:	For 2001, deadline extended for feature film scripts to August 30. All categories will have a permanent deadline of August 30 for 2002 and after.
Rules:	Scripts must be submitted in proper format; entries must be accompanied by the $25 entry fee and signed release form. Where the script was written by a partnership, both partners must submit a signed release form; entries must be postmarked by the deadline; writers offered fellowships will be required to relocate to Halifax for the duration of the fellowship; scripts will not be returned unless accompanied by a self-addressed stamped envelope with sufficient return postage.

Best Advice:	We are looking for commercial projects intended for the mass market. Good characterization, a strong series plotline and professionalism on the part of the writer are essential. Polish your dialogue and pay attention to format, spelling and grammar. We are using this program to develop professional caliber writers capable of delivering commercial scripts on-time and on-budget. For series entrants, don't forget to include your character summaries and one-page synopsis of the series plotline.
Director:	Natalie Durdle, director of The Animation Academy and writer/producer for Animatrix Productions.
Judges:	First round evaluations: The script will be evaluated for professionalism and structural elements. Scripts will be eliminated at this level for obvious lack of care with grammar, spelling and format. Additionally, bad dialogue, a lack of understanding the basics of writing a script and poor attention to detail will also cause a script to be eliminated. Second Round Evaluations: Students of the Production Management course at The Animation Academy as well as focus group volunteers will read the scripts for interest. This is not an elimination round. This score will be combined with the score from the Third Round Evaluations to come up with a list of semi-finalists. Third Round Evaluations: Distribution and Marketing staff from Animatrix Productions will evaluate the script for marketability. Semi-Finals and Finals: Evaluations will be done be a combined panel of producers, marketing and distribution staff from Animatrix Productions and industry distribution companies. Scripts will be reread for story structure and plot development and this score will be combined with a second evaluation for commercial viability. In the early years of the competition when there are expected to be fewer entries, these two stages may be combined into one.
Cash prizes:	First place in each age category for best concept: $1,000 (U.S.); three runners up in each category: $100 (U.S.).

Non-cash prizes: Fellowships of $20,000 (Canadian) plus accommodation and roundtrip airfare will be awarded. The numbers of fellowships offered will depend on the numbers of marketable projects we receive and the numbers of students in the third year Production Management course. Numbers will also be affected by the number of writers and projects we anticipate that we will need for the webcast line-up in the following year. Fellows will be required to relocate to Halifax, Nova Scotia for the duration of the 12-month program.

TIPS

for Series Search and Fellowship Entrants

For Series Search Entrants:

1. We're looking for series concepts that we can potentially spin out for two or three years if the viewers like it. Merchandizing potential is nice, but don't sacrifice a good character because he/she/it can't be turned into a stuffed animal or trading card. A solid series that has the viewer coming back each week is just as valuable.

2. If possible, get the script in as soon as possible. We will give each script the most honest read possible—after all, it's in our own best interest. But after about two hundred scripts, they are all going to start running together at some point. The more time we have to read the script, the better.

3. Our viewing market is primarily web-based. For the tweens (ages 8-13) and the teens (13-17) anything they would watch on TV stands a good chance of winning. The adult demographic is a bit tougher. Science fiction, horror and fantasy are always good bets. Well executed mystery/suspense also stands a good chance, as does a good solid comedy.

4. Avoid series concepts such as soap operas where the settings and actions are simply props to the physical portrayals and emotional angst of the actors. Animated characters are not capable of the same level of emotional portrayal using body language. Almost all of the subtext is lost unless replaced with

strong settings, music or dialogue. A series written for animation must rely more heavily on the story plotline and action/reaction to reveal character emotions and motivations.

5.   Consider your audience carefully when writing for our adult market. For the first few years, much of our general audience will be under 35. Those older than 35 will generally be of above average education, income and computer literate. Most will be professionals.

6.   We have no objections to sex or violence provided it is appropriate for the storyline. If the characters sleep together there better be a reason other than "just because." It doesn't have to be love, but it has to be true to the character.

7.   For writers of children's programming—no wicked stepmothers! It's cliché and socially irresponsible. Family relationships can be any combination providing there is some potential for a supportive, parental role by an adult at some point in the story arc.

For Fellowship entrants:
1.   Polish your scripts. Pay close attention to spelling, format and the basic rules of script rewriting. Our fellowship writers will be working writers—the script should be as professional as possible.

How does an animated script differ from a live-action script?
Over 55 percent of human communication can be attributed to visual body language. In addition, emotions are contagious. University studies have proven that people tend to reflect the emotional states of those around them. Those same studies have also shown that those people do not have to be in the same room. People shown photos of angry people began to display the physical characteristics of anger. This means that a skilled actor can reproduce an echo of what he or she is feeling through the use of body language. This physical involvement gives an immediacy to the performance, allowing us to experience catharsis and suspend disbelief.

An animated production cannot do this, at least, not with the same effectiveness. Animated characters can only display the broader body language cues, thus the audience does not react as strongly to the characters from a visual perspective and it becomes harder to suspend disbelief because you are not physically experiencing anger, sadness or joy to the same extent you would with live action. However, your audience knows what emotions they are supposed to be feeling and will willingly allow themselves to be swayed if you don't put any obstacles in their path.

Emotional subtext is enhanced in animation through the use of light and shadow more than body language. Use settings that make it easy to do. Settings that would be over the top or "B" grade special effects in live action can be used successfully in animation. Consider a ghostly breeze in an old attic. Live action, it's B grade horror or a quick shot to show the window isn't open. You get some shadow but you really can't play with the candle glow. Again, you're focused on how terrified the actor is. In animation you can show the glow of the candle as it advances, the changing colors of the old paneling, the graceful sway of the cobwebs—the setting that becomes the focus now, not the character. We know the character is scared silly—but we don't have to show it. An off-camera gasp and the candle flickering dangerously does it more effectively.

Make sure that the story, action or settings give the audience all the information they need to know what they are supposed to be feeling. Again, you can't rely on an actor's body language to tell them.

Lastly, polish that dialogue. On the nose dialogue, talking heads and trite phrases work against you in animation even more so than live action. Without the visual clues, everything else—including dialogue—becomes more important and the audience is less likely to ignore it if it sounds stupid. Because your audience is concentrating on visual clues they aren't as trained to see, don't distract them. Mountains of explanatory dialogue force them to concentrate on what the characters are saying rather than what they are doing. The emotional connection is more fragile, and if it gets broken it is harder to reestablish. If that happens, you have a bunch of people watching a bunch of pretty pictures instead of an involved audience happily making themselves feel what you've told them to feel.

SET IN PHILADELPHIA
SCREENWRITING COMPETITION

Purpose:	To promote quality film productions in Philadelphia and recognize excellence in screenwriting.
Entry fee:	$35
Year began:	1993
Categories:	Set primarily in Philadelphia area, all genres, all subjects.
Sponsor:	Philadelphia Film Office
Address:	Set In Philadelphia Screenwriting Competition International House 3701 Chestnut St. Philadelphia, PA 19104
Phone:	(215) 895-6593
Fax:	(215) 895-6562
Email:	sip@ihphilly.org
Website:	www.libertynet.org/pfwc/sip. (Prizes, judging, application, criteria, rules, sponsors, past judges, more)
Deadline:	January 25
Rules:	Material will not be returned. Do not send originals. Scripts between 85-130 pages.
Best Advice:	Write a terrific story. Get as much critical feedback as possible from people who are not your friends and family. Read the guidelines. The recognition that comes from winning a competition is at least as valuable as the cash reward.
Director:	David Haas
Judges:	Industry professionals evaluate visual quality, dramatic force, characters, plot/structure, dialogue and the extent to which the script tells a genuine Philadelphia story.
Cash prizes:	$5,000; $1,000 awarded to an outstanding writer under thirty (who has not previously won).
Non-cash prizes:	Readings, publicity, more.

SET IN TEXAS SCREENWRITING COMPETITION

Purpose:	To focus on the culture and the people of Texas.
Entry fee:	$25
Year began:	1998
Categories:	Tell a Texas story.
Sponsor:	Ancestral Films, Inc.
Address:	Set in Texas Screenwriting Competition Attn: Ancestral Films c/o Cultural Arts Council of Houston 3201 Allen Pkwy. #150 Houston, TX 77019
Phone:	(713) 527-9548
Email:	ancestrl@ancestralfilms.org
Website:	www.ancestralfilms.org
Deadline:	February 02 (biennial contest)
Rules:	Scripts should be between 30-120 pages. Submit four copies. Do not put your name on any part of the script. Include an entry form with contact information. (See website for more.)
Best Advice:	Avoid two-dimensional characters, characters who are too perfect. Life itself isn't flawless. Don't allow your stories to be too linear. Set the scene, time period and surroundings. Film is a visual medium, and it works best with metaphors and aesthetics. Don't get to engrossed in the mechanics. Sit back, relax and let your wisdom flow.
Director:	Mohammed Kamara, Executive Director.
Judges:	Ancestral Films and other professionals. Judges on artistic merit, texture and extent to which the script tells a genuine Texas story.
Cash prizes:	$1,500.
Non-cash prizes:	Publicity.

SHARE THE DREAM
ROMANTIC SCRIPTWRITING CONTEST

Purpose:	To find that great opening to a script!
Entry fee:	Scriptscene/RWA member $15, RWA member $20, Non-RWA member $25
Year began:	2000
Categories:	Romance
Sponsor:	Scriptscene/Romance Writers of America (RWA)
Address:	Share the Dream Contest c/o 510 1/2 E. Mulberry St. Bloomington, IL 61701
Email:	dixriter@aol.com
Website:	scriptscene.bizland.com/contest. (Contest form, prizes, more)
Deadline:	April 30
Rules:	Industry format. Send four copies of first 10-15 pages, no more. Do not count the title page. There should be an inciting incident in the entry. Include a SASE. Include a cover letter with the following: name, address, phone number, email address, RWA membership number. Author's name should not appear on any page but the title page.
Best Advice:	Follow the rules.
Director:	Dixie Schulz, Chairperson
Judges:	First round judged and critiqued by qualified Scriptscene/RWA members.
Cash prizes:	First place: $50, Second place: $25, Third place: $10.
Non-cash prizes:	Read by industry professionals.

SHENANDOAH PLAYWRIGHT'S RETREAT

Purpose:	To provide young and established writers a stimulating, challenging environment to test and develop new work in a safe haven, free from the pressures of everyday living. A four-week writing retreat.
Entry fee:	None
Year began:	1977
Categories:	All genres accepted.
Sponsor:	ShenanArts
Address:	Shenandoah Playwright's Retreat Pennyroyal Farm Rt. 5, Box 167-F Staunton, VA 24401
Phone:	(540) 248-1868
Fax:	(540) 248-7728
Email:	shenanarts@cfw.com
Deadline:	February 1
Rules:	Send two bound copies and a personal background statement or bio. Send SASE for return of script and/or stamped postcard for acknowledgement of submission.
Best advice:	We look for worldview. Do not send in supportive materials. Submit clean drafts, on time or early if possible. Send a clear statement of your background and experience, and what you hope to achieve during the retreat. Include a cast list, with character descriptions and sets. List your title, name, address, phone number on the title page. People in action and conflict are most interesting. Do not send in corrections.
Director:	Robert Graham Small
Judges:	Directors, dramaturgs and professional writers.
Non-cash prizes:	Full fellowships include room/board, transportation, collaboration with team of experts, feedback from advocates. Staged reading.
Success story:	The creative home for hundreds of writers from around the world.

SIR PETER USTINOV
TELEVISION SCRIPTWRITING AWARD

Purpose:	To recognize excellence in the writing of television programs for a family audience by a young scriptwriter who is a non-U.S. citizen living outside the U.S.
Entry fee:	None
Year began:	1997
Category:	Television (family audience)
Sponsor:	The International Council of NATAS Foundation
Address:	Sir Peter Ustinov Television Scriptwriting Award c/o The International Council of National Academy of Television Arts and Sciences 142 West 57th Street, 16th Floor New York, NY 10019
Phone:	(212) 489-6969
Fax:	(212) 489-6557
Email:	nancyck@iemmys2000.com
Website:	www.iemmys2000.com
Deadline:	September 1
Rules:	Submit a half-hour to one-hour English language television drama. Cannot be a U.S. citizen or resident. Must be under thirty years old. Include an entry form. May not have had a script produced for television prior to submission date. (See website for more.)
Best Advice:	The judges' decisions will be based on original story, dramatic situations and scenes, compelling characters and how they are developed, crisp, believable dialogue, and use of the visual medium.
Director:	Nancy Clark, Program Manager
Judges:	NATAS
Cash prizes:	$5,000.
Non-cash prizes:	Trip to New York to attend International Emmy Awards Gala.

SLAMDANCE SCREENPLAY COMPETITION

Purpose:	To promote new talent.
Entry fee:	Postmark by March 2 (early): $40, postmark by May 1: (main) $45, postmark by July 23 (final): $50
Year began:	1997
Categories:	Feature length—all genres.
Sponsor:	Screenplay.com
Address:	5634 Melrose Ave. Los Angeles, CA 90038
Fax:	(323) 466-1784
Email:	lhansen@slamdance.com
Website:	www.slamdance.com (Rules, FAQs, entry form, deadlines and fees)
Deadline:	July 23
Rules:	Use entry form on website. Cover should include title. Bind with brads. Include a one to three sentence synopsis, contact name, address, phone number. Material will not be returned. Not previously optioned, sold or produced, written in English. Cannot have received awards from other competitions. Length 70-140 pages. See website for complete rules and requirements.
Best Advice:	Write with passion and conviction. Screenplays will be scored on character development, story, dialogue, structure and originality.
Director:	Larry Hansen
Judges:	Industry readers and producers
Cash prizes:	$3,500.
Non-cash prizes:	Free coverage to all entrants.
Success story:	Over fifty production companies, studios and managers request to read our Top Twelve list. Many Slamdance finalists have consequently had screenplays produced or optioned, or obtained writing jobs as the direct result of the Slamdance Screenplay Competition.

SOCIETY FOR CINEMA STUDIES
STUDENT WRITING AWARD

Purpose:	To recognize students who show outstanding ability in the fields of film and television writing.
Entry fee:	Must be enrolled and must be members of SCS (contact SCS for member dues).
Categories:	Film or television studies
Sponsor:	The Society for Cinema Studies
Address:	Student Writing Award SCS Office, Film and Video Studies 302 Old Science Hall University of Oklahoma 640 Parrington Oval Norman, OK 73019-3060
Deadline:	September 30
Rules:	Must be enrolled in a recognized course in film and/or television studies at the time of submission. Must be members of SCS. Essay cannot have been previously published. One essay per student. Double-spaced, should not exceed 10,000 words. May submit double-sided copies. Author's name should not appear on or in the essay. Use a separate sheet for the following: name, address, essay title, and identification of particular course of study being pursued.
Best Advice:	Should be original works that significantly advance scholarship and thinking in the field of film and television studies.
Judges:	Scholastic committee
Cash prizes:	First place: $250, second place: $150, third place: $100.
Non-cash prizes:	First place is published in *Cinema Journal*.

SPLIT-SCREENPLAY CONTEST

Purpose:	To provide an avenue for writers to get unbiased feedback on their work.
Entry fee:	Free
Year began:	2000
Categories:	Feature Length Screenplays
Sponsor:	Diverve, Inc
Email:	info@screenplaycommunity.com
Website:	http://www.screenwriterscommunity.com
Deadline:	August
Rules:	Enter screenplay online in PDF format, review three other screenplays.
Director:	Chris Renzi
Judges:	All other contestants in a separate division from your screenplay.
Cash prizes:	$1,000 for first place. Final Draft software for second place.
Non-cash prizes:	Screenwriting software, paid professional review service.

SPLIT-SCREENPLAY CONTEST FAQs

Can I enter more than one screenplay?
Yes, but you will need to complete three reviews for each screenplay entered.

How can I convert my screenplay to PDF format?
Adobe has a free service to convert almost any document to PDF format. Click Adobe PDF to find out more.

Will I be able to choose additional scripts to review once I have completed my mandatory reviews?
No, in order to keep things as fair as possible, during the contest,

you will only be able to review assigned scripts. If you complete your three reviews, other scripts will be assigned to you, but it will not be mandatory for you to review them. After the contest, scripts will be available for all members to review.

If I enter more than one screenplay, will they be put into the same division?
Yes, if you enter more than one screenplay, they will all be entered into the same division; therefore, when reviewing screenplays, you still have an unbiased opinion, and it also avoids having the same wonderful screenwriter win both divisions.

Can I decline a selected screenplay to review?
No, the selections of the screenplays you must review are final.

Will I be able to read the reviews that were completed on my screenplay?
After the winners are announced on the site, all contestants will have the opportunity to read each review submitted for their screenplay for a small fee, to help keep site maintenance and ongoing support for future contests. Depending on the number of reviews submitted for a screenplay, the cost will be $7.95 for one review, $12.95 for two reviews and $16.95 for three or more reviews.

Can I include a title page with my entry that includes my name and contact information?
For the Split-Screenplay Contest, the option of leaving contact information with your screenplay is entirely up to the screenwriter. For purposes of judging, it is very unlikely that someone who knows you will be reviewing your screenplay. By leaving your contact information with your entry, the person reviewing it may someday be in a position to help you and thus will remember your name.

I have finished my three reviews for my entry and a fourth one has popped up. Is this one mandatory?
The fourth screenplay is optional. If you have entered more than one screenplay, you must complete three reviews for each one.

SQUARE MAGAZINE SCREENWRITING AWARD

Purpose: To find original voices in the screenwriting community and reward them with prizes, publicity and industry contacts.

Entry fee: Early: $30, Second deadline $40, Final: $50

Year began: 1998

Categories: Television and Film, all genres accepted.

Sponsor: *Square* magazine

Address: *Square* magazine Screenwriting Award
99 Park Ave.
New York, NY 10016

Phone: (212) 353-6021

Email: squaremag@aol.com

Website: www.squaremagazine.com
(References, participating production companies, more)

Deadline: Early: October 1-January 15, Second deadline February 15, Final: March 15 (2000 was extended to July 1)

Rules: Original work, not sold, produced or optioned. Multiple entries accepted. Collaborations accepted. Name, address, phone number must appear on title page. All pages must be numbered and in industry format. Any length, written in English. Material will not be returned. Do not send originals.

Best Advice: Forget about "advice to win!" Originality of plot and evidence of an original writing style always catches our judges' attention.

Director: Brian Christian

Judges: Industry professionals

Cash prizes: $2,000.

Non-cash prizes: Publicity, industry connections, feedback on all scripts.

SUNDANCE FEATURE FILM PROGRAM

Purpose:	To support original, compelling, human stories that reflect the independent vision of the writer.
Entry fee:	$30
Year began:	1980
Categories:	Feature films
Sponsor:	The Sundance Institute
Address:	The Sundance Institute 225 Santa Monica Blvd., 8th Floor Santa Monica, CA 90401
Phone:	(310) 394-4662
Fax:	(310) 394-8353
Email:	featurefilmprogram@sundance.org
Website:	www.sundance.org
Deadline:	First week of May
Rules:	Do not send the entire screenplay. Send the following: application, cover letter, resume/bio, synopsis (not to exceed two pages), first five pages of the script, entry fee.
Best Advice:	There are no specific do's or don'ts offered, just encouragement of the screenwriter's original vision.
Director:	Michelle Satter, Feature Film Program
Judges:	Feature Film Program
Non-cash prizes:	Participation in a residential lab, travel expenses, publicity.

TELLURIDE INDIEFEST

Purpose:	To showcase the best independent films and screenplays in the world.
Entry fee:	Varies—length of material, and date entered.
Year began:	1996
Categories:	All genres are acceptable.
Sponsor:	MJM Films and Queso Productions
Address:	P.O. Box 860 Telluride, CO 81435 (USA)
Phone:	(970) 728-3747
Fax:	(970) 728-8128
Email:	festival@tellurideindiefest.com
Website:	http://tellurideindiefest.com
Deadline:	August 1 (each year)
Rules:	Screenplays should not exceed 120 pages. Industry format.
Best Advice:	If you get 'em to giggle, you got 'em.
Director:	Michael Carr
Judges:	The Telluride community—proclaimed as being the most "film wise" on the planet.
Non-cash prizes:	Over 72 percent of our artists say they have significantly advanced their careers as a direct result of being selected by Telluride IndieFest.
Success story:	Every day above ground is a successful story.

ADVICE FROM THE TELLURIDE INDIE FEST

1. Follow the rules of each competition you enter. If a competition requests or even suggests that screenplays should be no more than 120 pages, do not send them a 150-page script.

2. Know your craft. Do not submit an improperly formatted screenplay to a competition. And, do not ever include any camera directions—as is the domain of the director, not the screenwriter. Just tell a great story in proper screenplay format. Buy the books and learn the craft.

3. Get used to rejection. If you cannot take rejection, you are in the wrong business. The strong, diligent and persevering survive the film business.

4. Write because you must write. If you have a passion to write, then write. The odds against selling a screenplay to Hollywood are staggering. It is a very competitive business and is very money-driven. Competitions do present opportunities for building a resume and track record of success; the recognition alone can open doors, but don't bank on it. If you truly are a writer, simply write because you have to.

5. Nothing beats a well-told story. Write something unique and refreshing. Ask yourself if your script can really be made into a movie. Is it cost-effective to make? Keep budget in mind.

TEXAS FILM INSTITUTE
ANNUAL SCREENPLAY COMPETITION

Purpose:	To find, evaluate and promote new screenwriters.
Entry fee:	$40 or $75 (with analysis).
Year began:	1999
Categories:	Drama, Comedy, Romantic Comedy, Action and Thriller, Animation, Family, Science Fiction
Sponsor:	Varies. This year's sponsors are New Line Cinema and Lions Gate Films.
Address:	409 Mountain Springs Dr. Boerne, Texas 78006
Phone:	(805) 537-5906
Email:	tfi@texasfilminstitute.com
Website:	www.texasfilminstitute.com
Deadline:	Varies, usually mid-March or April of each year
Rules:	On website, standard to industry.
Best advice:	Write original high-quality, character-driven stories.
Director:	Terri Spaugh
Judges:	Varies by year, for 2001: Marc Platt Productions, Imagemaker Films, Berg-Sacanni Productions are semifinal judges with New Line and Lions Gate as final judges.
Cash prizes:	A minimum of $1,000 in cash.
Non-cash prizes:	Full scholarship to Santa Fe Screenwriting conference, four months fees for writers script network, paid subscription to *Who's Buying What*, plus more annually.
Success story:	Two script sales, seven optioned screenplays, two agent/manager procurements in two years.

THREE PAGES SCREENPLAY COMPETITION

Purpose:	To help new and talented screenwriters make industry contacts and connections.
Entry fee:	$5
Year began:	2001
Categories:	One to three page original comedy scene.
Sponsor:	440 Films
Address:	2608 Second Avenue #286 Seattle, WA 98121
Phone:	(206) 464-9122
Website:	www.seemaxrun.com/threepages.htm
Deadline:	February 28 (check website for future contest dates).
Rules:	See website.
Director:	Max Adams
Non-cash prizes:	Top three entrants will receive a feature script read, referral and mentorship from author and award wining screenwriter Max Adams; publication on seemaxrun.com; and a signed copy of *The Screenwriter's Survival Guide* or *Guerilla Meeting Tactics and Other Acts of War* by Max Adams.

THUNDERBIRD FILMS SCREENPLAY COMPETITION

Purpose:	To discover and promote original screenplays. Dedicated to producing innovative and socially aware films of artistic excellence.
Entry fee:	$30
Year began:	1999
Categories:	Open to all writers.
Sponsor:	Thunderbird Films
Address:	Thunderbird Films 214 Riverside Dr. #112 New York, NY 10025
Phone:	(212) 352-4498
Email:	estannard@dekker.com
Website:	www.home.att.net/~thunderbirdfilms
Deadline:	March 30
Rules:	Scripts cannot have been optioned, sold or produced. Must be original work of author, or statement attesting to rights. Include the application form. Strongly suggest registering or copyrighting your work. Include a three-sentence synopsis.
Director:	Eric Stannard, Producer
Judges:	Thunderbird Films
Cash prizes:	$500.
Non-cash prizes:	Possible option.

TOP DOG PRODUCTIONS
SCREENPLAY COMPETITION

Purpose:	Industry exposure.
Entry fees:	Early: $30, Standard: $40, Third Notice $50, Final: $60
Categories:	All genres accepted.
Sponsor:	Top Dog Productions
Address:	Top Dog Productions Screenplay Competition 2567 E. Vermont Ave. Phoenix, AZ 85016
Phone:	(602) 840-6414
Email:	Topdogpro@aol.com
Website:	www.primenet.com/~topdogpr. (Deadlines, entry fees, rules, winners, entry form)
Deadlines:	Early: January 1, Standard: February 1, Third Notice March 1, Final: June 1.
Rules:	Include Entry form and Release, must own rights, written in English, 70-130 pages, multiple submissions accepted. Must not be optioned, produced or sold.
Judges:	Top Dog Productions
Cash prizes:	$5,000 total; first place: $3,000.
Non-cash prizes:	Publicity, contacts, software.

TROIKA MAGAZINE
STORY-TO-FILM COMPETITION

Purpose: To identify original short stories—fiction and nonfiction—with the potential to be developed for the film medium and assist in their screen adaptation.

Entry fee: $25

Categories: Fiction and nonfiction, any writer. Familiarity with screenplay format not required. 3000 word maximum synopsis.

Sponsor: *Troika* magazine

Address: *Troika* magazine Story-to-Film Competition
P.O. Box 1006
Weston, CT 06883

Phone: (203) 227-5377

Fax: (203) 222-9332

Email: contest@troikamagazine.com

Website: www.troikamagazine.com
(Rules, application, requirements, deadline, more)

Deadlines: February 28, May 31, August 30, October 30

Rules: English, max 3000 word synopsis, original work, not sold, produced or optioned. Include application form, entry fee, release and SASE for notification. (See website for more)

Best Advice: Follow the guidelines.

Director: Fran Samson, Managing Editor

Judges: Professional representatives in the film and screenwriting community.

Cash prizes: $250 (to top three).

Non-cash prizes: Publication in the magazine, option consideration, other gifts, subscription.

UCLA EXTENSION/DIANE THOMAS SCREENWRITING AWARDS

Purpose:	To introduce qualified screenwriting students to professionals in the industry.
Email:	writers@unex.ucla.edu
Year began:	1988
Categories:	Feature film scripts only. Writers must take three 3-unit screenwriting courses at the UCLA Extension, and entries are then developed in the Writer's Program screenwriting class.
Sponsor:	UCLA Writer's Program
Address:	Brandon Gannon/UCLA Writer's Program 10995 Le Conte Ave. #440 Los Angeles, CA 90024-2883
Phone:	(310) 206-1542
Fax:	(310) 206-7382
Website:	www.unex.ucla.edu/writers
Deadline:	January 27
Rules:	Submit two copies. Material will not be returned.
Best Advice:	Follow the rules. Pay attention to your application. No script changes allowed. Correct format required. Send your best.
Director:	Kathy Pomerantz, Program Representative
Judges:	UCLA Writer's Program
Cash prizes:	Contact contest.
Non-cash prizes:	Award ceremony, publicity, contact with agencies.

THE UNDEREXPOSED

Purpose:	To award, promote and celebrate writers who have yet to break into the industry.
Entry fee:	$30
Year began:	1999
Categories:	Feature length, all subjects—nothing is taboo or off limits.
Sponsor:	JOMO Productions
Address:	The Underexposed P.O. Box 15545 Boston, MA 02215
Phone:	(617) 713-3981
Email:	jomopro@yahoo.com
Website:	www.geocities.com/Hollywood/Highrise/8169
Deadline:	January 31
Rules:	Must not have been optioned, produced or sold for more than $1,000. 80-130 pages.
Best Advice:	Character development is very important. Write intriguing characters. Does not necessarily have to follow the A-B-C's of screenplay writing, but plot points should be logical.
Director:	John Morgan, President JOMO Productions
Judges:	JOMO Productions
Cash prizes:	First place: $4,000; second place: $1,000; third place: $500.
Non-cash prizes:	Publicity, industry contacts.

UNIQUE TELEVISION SCRIPT WRITING CONTEST

Purpose:	To find fresh writing talent for television, cable and emerging technologies.
Entry fee:	$45 (Satisfaction is guaranteed, see website for details.)
Year began:	1998
Categories:	Pilot scripts, MOWs, Internet Short, Spec of existing show—all genres accepted.
Sponsor:	Unique Television Script Writing Contest
Address:	Unique Television Script Writing Contest P.O. Box 22367 Eagan, MN 55122-0367
Email:	info@uniquetelevision.com
Website:	www.uniquetelevision.com (FAQs, application, guarantee, newsletter, winner's list, more)
Deadline:	June 1, December 1
Rules:	Multiple submissions accepted. Must be original work. No name, address, phone number, or any other identifying marks may appear anywhere on the script. Script title only on front page. Advise copyright or registration of material. Must be at least 18 years old. Material is not returned. (See website for more.)
Best Advice:	Write a well-written, commercially viable script. The June deadline generally receives fewer entries.
Director:	Lisa Germain
Judges:	Industry professionals.
Cash prizes:	Pilot script: $1,000; MOW: $1,000; Internet short: $200; Spec of existing show: $200.
Non-cash prizes:	Publicity, notes.

UPSTREAM PRODUCTIONS
BIANNUAL SCREENPLAY COMPETITION

Purpose:	To find passionate and sincere writers, true lovers of great film. We want to find those gifted writers who truly want to change the world; positive writers who were meant to be in this business. We're searching for honest, well-written scripts that need to get on the screen.
Entry fee:	$35
Year began:	1999
Categories:	Feature length only, all genres. (We're not saying we are anti-mainstream, but we are saying that mainstream films can be good or really, really bad.)
Sponsor:	Upstream Productions
Address:	16250 Ventura Blvd.#465 Encino, CA 91436
Phone:	(818) 752-3827
Fax:	(818) 528-2549
Email:	upstreamprod@mindspring.com
Website:	www.upstreamprod.com
Deadline:	Spring: March 1, Fall: September 1.
Rules:	Not sold or under option during time of contest. Use standard industry format. Only title should appear on the cover. Please include a second title sheet with your name, address, phone numbers. Submissions will not be returned. Substitutions will not be accepted, including new pages. Must be written in English. We suggest you register your material with the WGA. (See website for more.)
Best Advice:	Write from the heart and for yourself, not for an audience. Don't fake it. Come from the heart and write what you know and what you think is important. Don't think about the deal or your career or fame. These influence and poison a script. Keep it pure and people will drink it.
Director:	Young-Sun Kim

Judges:	Alternating industry professionals.
Cash prizes:	$1,000 grand prize.
Non-cash prizes:	Official announcements to agencies/studios. Website promotions.
Success story:	Gregory Johnson was our winner last fall.

> **"**Don't submit scripts in which the characters' dialogue all sounds alike. The top ten most common dialogue problems are: too obvious, too many one-liners, too repetitious, too long, too similar, too stilted, too preachy, too introspective, too inconsistent, too unbelievable.**"**
>
> —from *Television and Screenwriting: From Concept To Contract*
> by Richard A. Blum

VENICE ARTS SCREENWRITING COMPETITION

Purpose: To pursue the development of innovative screen-writing programs to support both the local community in Los Angeles and the worldwide community via the Internet. The screenwriting competition was established in response to various production companies requesting a conduit in which to identify and mentor new screenwriters.

Entry fee: $45

Year began: 2000

Categories: Feature-Length and Shorts

Sponsor: Final Draft Inc., Action/Cut Directed By Seminar, Robert McKee Story Seminar, Hollywood Creative Directory, Learning Annex, Hollywood Literary Sales, Writer's Script Network.

Address: 27636 Ynez Rd
L-7 No. 231
Temecula, CA 92591

Fax: (909) 494-4093

Email: contest@venicearts.com

Website: www.venicearts.com

Deadline: February 10

Rules: The competition is open to any writer without produced feature film credits. Full length screenplays must be within 90-130 pages, and shorts within 10-40 pages. Electronic entries are accepted and encouraged.

Best Advice: Know your screenplay formatting. Incorrect spelling, grammatical errors and sloppy formatting all red flag you as an amateur. Read one or more professional screenplays. Read at least two books on how to (or how NOT to) write a screenplay. The common denominators are plot, characterization, pacing and structure. Know the various paradigms. Choose one that resonates with you. Get other screenwriters to read your first draft. Find them in a local or online workshop.

Director:	James Woodward and Lisa James.
Judges:	Writer/Director/Producer Abbie Bernstein, Maryam Dalan (Drama Garage Screenplay Series), Michael Faulkner (Klasky Csupo Productions), Director/Producer Marla Friedler, Shari Hamrick (Alianza Films International), Melody Jackson (Smart Girls Productions, Inc.), Jeremy Kleiner (KPE Films), Sandy Mackey (Quillco Agency), Robyn Meisinger (Radmin Co.), Sally Merlin (*Scr(i)pt* magazine, former UCLA faculty member), Lenny Minelli (A Picture of You Agency), Vin Morreale Jr. (VSM Productions), Wendi Niad (Niad Management), Marilyn Pesola (Last Writes Literary Consulting), Anna Piazza (Chadwick and Gros Literary Agency), Robert Schaefer (veteran screenwriter and producer), Amy Taylor (Cedar Grove Literary Agency) and Carole Western (Montgomery West Literary Agency). Judges vary according to availability.
Cash prizes:	Full Length: $1,000, $500 and $100 to first, second and third place. Short: $500.
Non-cash prizes:	Final Draft screenwriting Software, Action/Cut Directed By seminar, Robert McKee Story Seminar, Hollywood Creative Directory's Producers Directory, plus various screenwriting books.
Success story:	2000 first place winners Walt Ulbricht and Ron Berger have a director attached to *The Promise*. 2000 third place winner *Night Blooming Jasmine* will be performed April 25 by Hollywood's Drama Garage—an invitation-only event. The winning screenplays have been requested by many of Hollywood's most eminent producers and agents.

VIRGINIA GOVERNOR'S SCREENWRITING COMPETITION

Purpose: To give Virginia screenwriters the opportunity to have their work evaluated and promoted.

Entry fee: None

Year began: 1986

Categories: General

Sponsor: Virginia Film Office

Address: Virginia Film Office Screenwriting Competition
                Riverfront Plaza West Tower, 19th Fl.
                901 East Byrd St.
                Richmond, VA 23219-4048

Phone: (804) 371-8205 or (800) 854-6233

Fax: (804) 371-8177

Email: vafilm@virginia.org

Website: www.film.virginia.org

Deadline: June 8

Rules: Only open to residents of Virginia. At least 75 percent of the script must use Virginia locations. One submission per author. 80-120 pages.

Best Advice: Don't copy mediocre Hollywood scripts. Write what you know and care about and proofread carefully.

Director: Rita McClenny

Judges: First round: industry professionals, second round: working professionals.

Cash prizes: $1,000.

Success story: Vince Gilligan was an early winner of the competition. He has had two films made: *Greater Napalm* and *Home Fries*, is a writer and executive producer on *X-Files*, and has his own production deal.

WALT DISNEY STUDIOS/
ABC WRITERS FELLOWSHIP

Purpose:	To find ethnically diverse writers for purposes of employment. Looking for up to eight culturally and ethnically diverse writers to work full-time developing their craft at Disney and ABC.
Entry fee:	None
Year began:	1989
Categories:	Film and Television. Open to culturally and ethnically diverse writers.
Sponsor:	Walt Disney Studios, ABC-TV
Address:	Fellowship Program Admin. Walt Disney Studios/ABC Writers Fellowship 500 S. Buena Vista St. Burbank, CA 91521-0705
Phone:	(818) 560-6894
Website:	www.members.tripod.com/~disfel/index. (Application, instructions, FAQs, recommended reading)
Deadline:	May 1-May 21
Rules:	One application to either category, not both. Need to relocate to Los Angeles area. Television category accepts a full-length, live-action, half-hour or hour script, based on any current comedy or drama series. (See website for more.)
Best Advice:	Read the instructions and follow them. Use professional format. Study produced scripts. Register your work.
Director:	Troy Nethercott, Program Director
Judges:	Disney/ABC
Cash prizes:	$33,000 salary for one year.
Non-cash prizes:	Publicity; writers chosen outside Los Angeles will be provided with transportation and one month's accommodations.
Success story:	Many television staff positions, feature writing assignments.

WARNER BROS. COMEDY WRITERS WORKSHOP

Purpose: To develop talented sitcom writers. A ten-week residency program in Burbank, CA.

Entry fee: $25 application fee. (The cost to participate in the workshop is $495)

Year began: 1977

Categories: Situation comedy

Sponsor: Warner Bros.

Address: Warner Bros. Comedy Writers Workshop
300 Television Plaza
Burbank, CA 91505

Phone: (818) 954-7906

Email: sitcomwksp@aol.com

Deadline: October 21

Rules: Sample script based on a half-hour comedy that has aired during the previous season. Include a one-page resume and/or bio. Writing teams are acceptable.

Best Advice: Submit your best work. Write a smart, funny, character-driven spec script. Not for beginners. The program, more a showcase for professionals, is designed to find staff-ready writers.

Director: Jack Gilbert

Judges: Industry professionals

Non-cash prizes: Development deals, staff positions.

Success story: Over a hundred alumni have gone to work on sitcoms or features.

THE WASHINGTON STATE
SCREENPLAY COMPETITION

Purpose:	To promote scripts written for Washington State
Entry fee:	$35
Year began:	1997
Categories:	Feature division and short film division.
Sponsor:	The Washington State Film Office, Alaska Airlines, Final Draft, Inc., Tully's Coffee, Washington Media Producers Council, See-Through Films
Address:	2001 Sixth Avenue #2600 Seattle, WA 98121
Phone:	(206) 956-3205
Fax:	(206) 728-8530
Email:	Wafilm@cted.wa.gov
Website:	www.wafilm.wa.gov
Deadline:	December 10, 2001
Rules:	Feature Division: 75 percent of the script must be set in Washington State. First round is a synopsis and the best ten consecutive pages of your script. Short Division: Five pages or less and 100 percent of the script must be set in Washington State.
Best Advice:	Keep writing and entering contests!
Director:	Suzy Kellett, Director; Kristina Erickson, Manager
Judges:	Prominent directors, producers and agents
Cash prizes:	Winners in each division receive $1,500.
Non-cash prizes:	Round trip plane ticket, Final Draft Scriptwriting software, Tully's coffee and the opportunity to be read by experts.
Success story:	Our 1999 winner sold one of his screenplays to Columbia Pictures and it is now in prep to film this year.

WATKINS INTERNATIONAL
SCREENPLAY COMPETITION

Purpose:	To celebrate the most creative and innovative in independent film production. To further independent-minded filmmaking.
Entry fee:	$25
Year began:	1995
Categories:	Open to anyone. All genres accepted.
Sponsor:	Watkins Film School
Address:	Watkins International Screenplay Competition 100 Powell Pl. Nashville, TN 37204
Phone:	(615) 356-0953
Email:	robrien@bellsouth.net
Deadline:	January 31
Rules:	Industry format. Writing teams are acceptable. No limit to number of scripts entered per author. Must be original work, not previously produced. Include a detailed one to two page synopsis (very important). Submit a cover sheet with each script (name, address, phone number). Prefer 105-120 pages, bound. Do not include author's name anywhere on the manuscript. Submissions should include: script, synopsis, cover sheet and entry fee. Scripts will not be returned.
Best Advice:	Correctly formatted scripts win. Failing scripts do so because they don't engage the reader. Scripts also fail because they have extraordinary plot problems or are filled with characters to which the reader cannot relate. Read scripts of produced independent films as a guide.
Director:	Randy O'Brien, Chair

Judges:	Watkins Film School faculty/staff. Judging is assessed on overall creativity, freshness of premise, presence of a truly meaningful theme, originality and depth of characters, clearly-defined but non-conventional conflict, authenticity of dialogue, original story development, innovative methods of storytelling, coherence of overall structure and professionalism of presentation.
Cash prizes:	First place: $1,000; second place: $500; third place: $250; fourth place $150; fifth place $100.
Non-cash prizes:	Top ten scripts are made available to producers, directors and motion picture industry executives.
Success story:	Past winners have signed with agents, managers and have had work optioned.

TIPS

from *How NOT To Write A Screenplay*
by Denny Martin Flinn

SCREENPLAY
A screenplay is like a crossword puzzle. Not only do you need the right word, you need the word with the right number of letters.

TITLES
There is no good or bad advice about titles, because there are no good or bad titles. If you write a good movie, everyone will remember your title.

COVER LETTER
Don't rave about your own screenplay. Don't cast it. Don't tell us how commercial it is.

CONTINUED
Don't use (CONTINUED) at the top and bottom of each page. Anyone reading your screenplay who doesn't know how to turn the page is a numbskull.

GOING CRAZY
Too many CAPITAL LETTERS tend to DRIVE the READER a little CRAZY. Too many stage directions drive actors crazy, and nobody ever follows them anyway.

SPECIAL EFFECTS
Don't put in special visual effects. Just say what happens, and let the SFX supervisor figure out how.

MECHANICS
Don't make grammatical errors, syntactical errors or errors of definition. Don't make spelling and typo errors.

THINK VISUAL
Don't write what can't be photographed. We don't know what we can't see.

REPETITION
If you've already told the audience, don't have the characters tell each other.

WESTCHESTER COUNTY FILM FESTIVAL

Purpose:	To promote and encourage Westchester County filmmakers.
Entry fee:	$25 per screenplay
Year began:	2000
Categories:	Features, Documentary Features, Documentary Short, Student, Works-in-Progress
Sponsor:	Westchester City Film Office and
Address:	148 Martine Ave. #107 White Plains, New York 10601
Fax:	(914) 995-2948
Email:	ii53@westchestergov.com/filmoffice
Website:	westchestergov.com/filmoffice
Deadline:	January 15
Rules:	All entries must have a bona fide connection to Westchester County. Any one of the following conditions will satisfy entry requirements for screenplays: 1) The screenplay is written by a Westchester County resident, and/or the screenplay's storyline is set in Westchester County.
Judges:	Rotating panel, changes annually.
Non-cash prizes:	Crystal Award

WILLIAMSPORT FILM AND VIDEO COLLECTIVE SCRIPT WRITING COMPETITION

Purpose:	To find good material for future production. A great opportunity for students, amateurs and novice writers.
Entry fee:	Feature $15, Short $10, Local Interest $5.
Categories:	Feature, Short, Local Interest
Sponsor:	Williamsport Film and Video Collective (non-profit organization), Changeworks
Address:	Film and Video Collective c/o Changeworks 445 Market St. #2 Williamsport, PA 17701
Phone:	(570) 326-7670
Email:	wfvc@hotmail.com
Deadline:	December 31
Rules:	Features 110 pages or less. Shorts 45 pages or less. Local Interest (i.e. Williamsport) no specified length. No treatments. Material will not be returned unless accompanied by SASE.
Director:	David Folmar, Founder
Judges:	WFVC
Non-cash prizes:	Awards reception, possible production.

from *This Business Of Screenwriting* by Ron Suppa, Esq.

WRITING
Allow the artist in you to create before the critic in you destroys. On the other hand, never submit your work until it is ready.

LOW-BUDGET GUIDELINES
- Character-driven stories
- Limited locations
- No complex stunts
- Day preferable to night
- Interior preferable to exterior
- No special effects
- No children or pets
- No period pieces
- Stick to terra firma
- No complex crowd shots
- Be realistic

PROTECTING YOUR WORK
- Submit wisely
- Maintain a paper trail
- Copyright your written work
- Register your work with the Writers Guild

RIGHTS
And never—under any circumstances and notwithstanding flattery or rosy promises—sign anything that could be construed to sell or transfer the rights to your "winning entry" without first consulting a good contract lawyer.

THE DEAL, PART I
The deal memo is a written confirmation of the fundamental terms of any purchase or employment agreement. While giving the appearance of an informal letter (often only one or two pages long), the deal memo is a binding agreement between the parties and governs all later writings on the subject.

THE DEAL, PART II
In an option agreement, the writer receives a fraction of the agreed-upon purchase price in exchange for granting the producer the exclusive right, over a given period of time (the option period), to rewrite, package and/or make the financial arrangements for the production of the material.

SIX LAWS OF THE SCREENWRITER'S CAREER
- The Law of Rejection: Don't let rejection dissolve your resolve.
- The Law of Change: There is no job security in Hollywood.
- The Law of Changes: We all have to make them.
- The Law of Birth: Keep those babies coming.
- The Law of Burying the Dead: Gulp and move on.
- The Law of Survival: Don't quit your day job.

WISCONSIN SCREENWRITERS FORUM
SCREENWRITERS CONTEST

Purpose:	To assist television and feature film scriptwriters through education, support and networking.
Entry fee:	Members $30, Non-members $60 (includes a one-year membership)
Year began:	1982
Categories:	Feature film or TV Movie, Television
Sponsor:	Wisconsin Screenwriters Forum (WSF is a nonprofit organization).
Address:	WSF Screenwriters Contest P.O. Box 11378 Milwaukee, WI 53211
Phone:	(888) 282-6776
Email:	wsf@execpc.com
Website:	www.execpc.com/~wsf (Deadline, categories, requirements, fee, judging, prizes, release form, more)
Deadline:	October 1
Rules:	Feature films must be between 90-120 pages. Episodic scripts are limited to a maximum of 75 pages. Do not send in before September 1. Include release form. Send three copies and a one page synopsis, in 12-point type. Cannot have been produced, sold or optioned prior to entering. Do not send originals.
Best Advice:	Use correct format. Careful of typos. Do not overwrite. Keep camera directions to a minimum—don't direct on paper.
Judges:	Wisconsin Screenwriters Forum
Non-cash prizes:	Certificates, subscriptions, tuition to a Los Angeles seminar, publicity, contacts.

THE 34TH ANNUAL WORLDFEST-HOUSTON INTERNATIONAL FILM FESTIVAL

Purpose: To honor creative excellence of Indie filmmakers and writers.

Entry fee: $45 to $90

Year began: 1968 (We are the oldest Film Festival in North America operating under the same management team.)

Categories: Screenplays, teleplays, feature films, short films, TV commercials, student, documentary, new media, radio, print, experimental, music videos

Sponsor: NEA, City of Houston, State of Texas, Kodak, Microsoft, Continental Airlines, Houston Chronicle, Houston press, ASU, Budget Rent-A-Car, LightSpeed computers, Houston Film Commission, Houston Film Society, more.

Address: P.O. Box 56566
                    Houston, Texas 77256

Fax: (713) 965-9960

Email: worldfest@aol.com

Website: www.worldfest.org (not .com)

Deadline: Dec 15 and Jan 15

Rules: Lots of rules, see the website.

Best Advice: A good story, well told!

Director: Kathleen Haney, Program Director, Hunter Todd, Executive Director

Judges: Twelve categories; a jury in each category.

Cash prizes: For student films, short films, screenplays: $1,000 and up.

Non-cash prizes: Remi Statue for grand award, Platinum, Gold, Silver and Bronze medals.

Success story: All winners in screenplays and shorts are submitted to the top 100 agents and producers in Los Angeles and New York. Each year several scripts are optioned and produced. Todd Robinson's Grand Prize winner *White Squall* was directed by WorldFest award winner Ridley Scott. *The Schooner* was optioned for production by producer Leigh Murray and is in pre-production.

> **"**Happy endings sell. Most of Hollywood hates unhappy endings.**"**
>
> —from *Screenwriting 434*
> by Lew Hunter

> **"**Is the central question of the movie answered?**"**
>
> —from *How To Write A Movie In 21 Days*
> by Viki King

> **"**Write up endings.**"**
>
> —from *Screenplay: The Foundations of Screenwriting*
> by Syd Field

WRITEMOVIES.COM

Purpose:	To find the best new screenplays, novels, short stories and articles.
Entry fee:	$29 early, $39 late; books: $49.
Year began:	2000
Categories:	Open to anyone. We consider material in English, French and German.
Sponsor:	Final Draft and others.
Address:	12228 Venice Blvd. # 539 Los Angeles, CA 90066
Fax:	(310) 397-3695
Email:	Write@WriteMovies.com
Website:	www.WriteMovies.com
Deadline:	Three contests a year.
Rules:	No "shopped" material. Material will not be returned. See website for more.
Best Advice:	Read the suggested books. Get the material in early so readers have time to spend with it. Our taste is firmly grounded in the 1970s. We like stories in which the writer has something to say, and is not just going for the laugh or cheap thrill. We don't go crazy over wildly offbeat material. We're not thrilled with B-Movie cops-and-robbers stuff either. We're looking for something that has a unique, powerful lead; something that will make some star fall in love with it and get a studio to make it.
Director:	Alex Ross, Founder
Judges:	Industry professionals.
Cash prizes:	$2,500.
Non-cash prizes:	Submission of winners to high ranking executives at studios, production companies and agencies.
Success story:	From our first contest, one project optioned, principal photography to begin early next year. Others have gotten interest from major companies (Kennedy/Marshall) and agencies (the winners are still being submitted at time of writing).

8TH ANNUAL WRITERS NETWORK SCREENPLAY & FICTION COMPETITION

Purpose:	To give new and talented writers across the globe the chance to pursue a career in film, television and/or literary.
Entry fee:	$35—may submit two screenplays, teleplays or one novel or novel in progress.
Year began:	1993
Categories:	Screenplay, Teleplay, Play, Novel
Sponsor:	The Writers Network
Address:	289 S. Robertson Blvd., Ste 465 Beverly Hills, CA 90211
Phone:	(310) 275-0287
Email:	writersnet@aol.com
Website:	www.fadeinonline.com
Deadline:	May 15
Rules:	Material not under option or sold.
Best Advice:	Follow the guidelines!!!
Director:	Audrey Kelly
Judges:	Agents from ICM, William Morris, APA, AMG, Endeavor.
Cash prizes:	Up to $2,000.
Non-cash prizes:	Literary representation.
Success story:	Matt Healy, *Clay Pigeons* (Gramercy); Jon Bokenkamp, Preston Tylk, 2-picture deal; Haven Turleygood, *Irish*, deals with Joel Silver and Arnold Kopelson—all signed to ICM and Endeavor agencies.

WRITESAFE PRESENT-A-THON

Purpose:	To reward excellence in those who register their creative work with WriteSafe.com
Entry fee:	The Present-A-Thon is free to all those who protect their work by registering their files with WriteSafe.com and have it posted publicly for others to see.
Year began:	2000
Categories:	There are no categories. It is open to all creative material, including art (cartoons, drawings, paintings), writing (long and short fiction, poetry, collections, essays, television scripts, film scripts), games, music (music and lyrics), etc.
Sponsor:	WriteSafe.Com
Address:	Cloud Creek Ranch 422 West Carlisle Road Westlake Village, CA 91361
Phone:	(805) 495-3659
Fax:	(805) 495-0099
Email:	admin@writesafe.com
Website:	http://www.writesafe.com
Deadline:	The end of every quarter
Rules:	Entrants must register and post their work publicly on WriteSafe to be eligible.
Best Advice:	Write with energy, feeling and knowledge of the medium.
Director:	J.L. Manns
Judges:	J.L. Manns and the WriteSafe staff

Non-cash prizes: Guaranteed to be read by a panel of experts, including television network executives, production company executives, publishing executives, agents, game company executives, etc. (names available at the website); Final Draft software; StoryCraft software; ClickBook software; Sophocles Software; free entry into the Moondance Film Festival screen or television writing competition; subscription to *ScreenTalk* magazine; free registrations at WriteSafe.

Success story: Winners and entrants alike have sold their work or gotten jobs; one honorable Mmntion screenplay writer has had his film idea financed and put into production; a first place winner for Art has been offered a job as an illustrator on a magazine edited by a member of the panel of experts, etc.

> **"**The more a writer relies on flashbacks, the more he or she intrudes on the forward thrust of the plot.**"**
>
> —from *Television and Screenwriting: From Concept To Contract* by Richard A. Blum

(Except for the biggest money-maker in movie history, *Titanic*.)

THOUGHTS FROM A SCREENPLAY CONTEST DIRECTOR

by Eric Edson, Executive Director
of the Hollywood Symposium

The most common recurring script problems:

1. Passive heroes. Heroes must take constant action, be the architects of their own destiny, not merely be acted upon by others. They cannot be mere observers. They must have a strong goal at the start of the movie and pursue it relentlessly until the end. Your lead character should be the focus and driving energy behind every scene. They must display some form of courage at the start of your movie and thereby become special to the audience. An average Jane or Joe, unsure of herself or himself or of what they want to the point that they take no special action, can't carry a movie as the lead. And protagonists who feel sorry for themselves don't work, either. Your hero must be sympathetic, or at the very least empathetic, even if they are seriously flawed as people.

2. It is essential to have a strong, ongoing antagonist working to foil your hero's plans and desires throughout the film. This is the basis of rising conflict. You've got to have it. And no, your script is not the single exception to this rule. Without a looming and seemingly insurmountable antagonist, there is no conflict.

3. Movies must move. A string of lengthy dialogue scenes—no matter how brilliant the dialogue—do not constitute an effective film. If you envision a screenplay that is mostly people talking, try writing a play.

4. Screenplays require strong, active stories. This is the hardest element of the craft, creating that ever evolving, ever surprising, changing and twisting story.

5. A screenplay story must be believable within its own created reality. The world you build must convince us with its true-to-life details that it could, in fact, exist. And this is just as true of a domestic drama as science fiction. Whatever your setting, make it real.

6. Be careful of writing a dialogue scene that runs four pages long or more. Not that it's never done, just that your story justification had better be iron clad. The single most consistent scene

weakness is run-on dialogue. Every line of dialogue in your script must be meaningful and charged with conflict. Cut the needless dialogue, and a great many scenes will shrink 30-40 percent. Don't rely on dialogue to fill gaps in a thin plot.

7. The stakes in your movie must be very, very high. High stakes create urgency and tension. High stakes involve the audience. If not literal life or death, your stakes must be metaphorical life or death. Life or death of the soul.

APPENDIX

ENTERTAINMENT INDUSTRY RESOURCE GUIDE

ACADEMY PLAYERS DIRECTORY
8949 Wilshire Blvd.
Beverly Hills, CA 90211
Phone 310-247-3000
Fax 310-550-5034
URL www.playersdirectory.com

**ACTORS EQUITY ASSOCIATION
(AEA-CHI)**
203 N. Wabash Ave., Ste. 1700
Chicago, IL 60601
Phone 312-641-0393
Fax 312-641-6365
URL www.actorsequity.org

**ACTORS EQUITY ASSOCIATION
(AEA-LA)**
5757 Wilshire Blvd., Ste. 1
Los Angeles, CA 90036
Phone 323-634-1750
Fax 323-634-1777
URL www.actorsequity.org

**ACTORS EQUITY ASSOCIATION
(AEA-NY)**
165 W. 46th St., 15th Fl.
New York, NY 10036
Phone 212-869-8530
Fax 212-719-9815
URL www.actorsequity.org

**ACTORS EQUITY ASSOCIATION
(AEA-SF)**
235 Pine St., Ste. 1200
San Francisco, CA 94104
Phone 415-391-3838
Fax 415-391-0102
URL www.actorsequity.org

**ACTORS EQUITY ASSOCIATION
(AREA LIAISON LINES)**
Atlanta
404-257-2575

Austin/San Antonio	512-326-7648
Baltimore/D.C.	202-722-7350
Boston	617-720-6048
Buffalo/Rochester	716-883-1767
Cleveland	440-779-2001
Dallas/Fort Worth	214-922-7843
Denver	720-377-0072
Detroit	248-788-6118
Florida-Central	407-345-9322
Florida-South	305-460-5880
Houston	713-917-4564
Kansas City	816-926-9293
Las Vegas	702-452-4200
Milwaukee/Madison	414-963-4023
Minneapolis/St. Paul	612-924-4044
Philadelphia	215-966-1895
Phoenix/Tucson	602-265-7117
Pittsburgh	412-481-0816
San Diego	619-858-0055
St. Louis	314-851-0906
Seattle	425-637-7332

**ACTORS EQUITY ASSOCIATION
(AUDITION HOTLINES)**
Chicago
312-641-0418

Los Angeles	323-634-1776
New York City	212-869-1242
San Francisco	415-434-8007

ACTORS FUND OF AMERICA (CHI)
203 N. Wabash Ave., Ste. 2104
Chicago, IL 60601
Phone 312-372-0989
Fax 312-372-0272
URL www.actorsfund.org

ACTORS FUND OF AMERICA (LA)
5757 Wilshire Blvd., Ste. 400
Los Angeles, CA 90036
Phone 323-933-9244
Fax   323-933-7615
URL   www.actorsfund.org

ACTORS FUND OF AMERICA (NY)
729 Seventh Ave., 10th Fl.
New York, NY 10019
Phone 212-221-7300
Fax   212-764-0238
URL   www.actorsfund.org

ACTORS' WORK PROGRAM (LA)
5757 Wilshire Blvd., Ste. 400
Los Angeles, CA 90036-3635
Phone 323-933-9244
Fax   323-933-7615

ACTORS' WORK PROGRAM (NY)
165 W. 46th St., 16th Fl.
New York, NY 10036
Phone 212-354-5480 (ext. 50)
Fax   212-921-4295

**AMERICAN FEDERATION OF
MUSICIANS (AFM-LA)**
7080 Hollywood Blvd., Ste. 1020
Los Angeles, CA 90028
Phone 323-461-3441
Fax   323-462-8340
URL   www.afm.org

**AMERICAN FEDERATION OF
MUSICIANS (AFM-NY)**
1501 Broadway, Ste. 600
New York, NY 10036
Phone 212-869-1330
Fax   212-764-6134
URL   www.afm.org

**AMERICAN FEDERATION OF
TELEVISION & RADIO ARTISTS
(AFTRA-LA)**
5757 Wilshire Blvd., Ste. 900
Los Angeles, CA 90036-3689
Phone 323-634-8100
Fax   323-634-8246
URL   www.aftra.org

**AMERICAN FEDERATION OF
TELEVISION & RADIO ARTISTS
(AFTRA-NY)**
260 Madison Ave., 7th Fl.
New York, NY 10016
Phone 212-532-0800
Fax   212-545-1238
URL   www.aftra.org

**AMERICAN GUILD OF VARIETY
ARTISTS (AGVA-LA)**
4741 Laurel Canyon Blvd. Ste. 208
North Hollywood, CA 91607
Phone 818-508-9984
Fax   818-508-3029
Email agvala@earthlink.net
URL   home.earthlink.net/~agvala/

**AMERICAN GUILD OF VARIETY
ARTISTS (AGVA-NY)**
184 Fifth Ave., 6th Fl.
New York, NY 10010
Phone 212-675-1003
Fax   212-633-0097
Email agvany@aol.com
URL   home.earthlink.net/~agvala/

**AMERICAN SOCIETY OF COMPOSERS,
AUTHORS & PUBLISHERS (ASCAP-CHI)**
1608 W. Belmont Ave., Ste. 202
Chicago, IL 60657
Phone 773-472-1157
Fax   773-472-1158
URL   www.ascap.com

AMERICAN SOCIETY OF COMPOSERS, AUTHORS & PUBLISHERS (ASCAP-LA)
7920 Sunset Blvd., 3rd Fl.
Los Angeles, CA 90046
Phone 323-883-1000
Fax 323-883-1049
URL www.ascap.com

AMERICAN SOCIETY OF COMPOSERS, AUTHORS & PUBLISHERS (ASCAP-NY)
One Lincoln Plaza
New York, NY 10023
Phone 212-621-6000
Fax 212-724-9064
URL www.ascap.com

AMERICAN SOCIETY OF COMPOSERS, AUTHORS & PUBLISHERS (ASCAP-TN)
2 Music Square West
Nashville, TN 37203
Phone 615-742-5000
Fax 615-742-5020
URL www.ascap.com

THE AMERICAN SOCIETY OF YOUNG MUSICIANS
9244 Wilshire Blvd., Ste. 201
Beverly Hills, CA 90212
Phone 310-285-9744
Fax 310-285-9770
Email trielite@cs.com

ASSOCIATION OF AUTHORS' REPRESENTATIVES, INC. (AAR)
P.O. Box 237201, Ansonia Station
New York, NY 10003
Phone 212-252-3695
URL www.aar-online.org

ASSOCIATION OF TALENT AGENTS (ATA)
9255 Sunset Blvd., Ste. 930
Los Angeles, CA 90069
Phone 310-274-0628
Fax 310-274-5063
Email agentassoc@aol.com
URL www.agentassociation.com

BOOK PUBLICISTS OF SOUTHERN CALIFORNIA
6464 Sunset Blvd., #755
Hollywood, CA 90028
Phone 323-461-3921
Fax 323-461-0917

BROADCAST MUSIC, INC. (BMI-FL)
5201 Blue Lagoon Dr., Ste. 310
Miami, FL 33126
Phone 305-266-3636
Fax 305-266-2442
URL www.bmi.com

BROADCAST MUSIC, INC. (BMI-LA)
8730 Sunset Blvd., 3rd Fl. West
Los Angeles, CA 90069-2211
Phone 310-659-9109
Fax 310-657-6947
URL www.bmi.com

BROADCAST MUSIC, INC. (BMI-LONDON)
84 Harley House, Mary Lebone Rd.
London NW1 5HN England
Phone 011-44-171-486-2036
URL www.bmi.com

BROADCAST MUSIC, INC. (BMI-NY)
320 W. 57th St.
New York, NY 10019-3790
Phone 212-586-2000
Fax 212-489-2368
URL www.bmi.com

BROADCAST MUSIC, INC. (BMI-TN)
10 Music Square East
Nashville, TN 37203-4399
Phone 615-401-2000
Fax 615-401-2707
URL www.bmi.com

CASTING SOCIETY OF AMERICA (CSA)
606 N. Larchmont Blvd., Ste. 4B
Los Angeles, CA 90004-1309
Phone 323-463-1925
URL www.castingsociety.com

**DIRECTORS GUILD OF AMERICA
(DGA-CHI)**
400 N. Michigan Ave., Ste. 307
Chicago, IL 60611
Phone 312-644-5050
Fax 312-644-5776
URL www.dga.org

**DIRECTORS GUILD OF AMERICA
(DGA-LA)**
7920 Sunset Blvd.
Los Angeles, CA 90046
Phone 310-289-2000
      323-851-3671 (Agency Listing)
Fax 310-289-2029
URL www.dga.org

**DIRECTORS GUILD OF AMERICA
(DGA-NY)**
110 W. 57th St.
New York, NY 10019
Phone 212-581-0370
Fax 212-581-1441
URL www.dga.org

DRAMATISTS GUILD OF AMERICA
1501 Broadway, Ste. 701
New York, NY 10036
Phone 212-398-9366
URL www.dramaguild.com

**HISPANIC ORGANIZATION OF
LATIN ACTORS**
Clemente Soto Velez Cultural Center
107 Suffolk St., Ste. 302
New York, NY 10002
Phone 212-253-1015
Fax 212-253-9651
Email holagram@aol.com
URL www.hellohola.org

**THE MULTICULTURAL MOTION
PICTURE ASSOCIATION (MMPA)**
9244 Wilshire Blvd.
Beverly Hills, CA 90212
Phone 310-285-9743
Fax 310-285-9770
Email trielite@cs.com

**NATIONAL ASSOCIATION OF
TALENT REPRESENTATIVES**
c/o The Gage Group
315 W. 57th St., Ste. 4H
New York, NY 10019
Phone 212-262-5696
Fax 212-799-6718

**NATIONAL CONFERENCE OF
PERSONAL MANAGERS (NCOPM-CA)**
6680 Alhambra Ave., Ste. 507
Martinez, CA 94553
Phone 818-762-NCPM
URL www.ncopm.com

**NATIONAL CONFERENCE OF
PERSONAL MANAGERS (NCOPM-NY)**
46-19 220th Pl.
Bayside, NY 11361-3654
Phone 718-225-5103
Email ncopm@aol.com
URL www.cybershowbiz.com/ncopm

PRODUCERS GUILD OF AMERICA (PGA)
6363 Sunset Blvd., 9th Fl.
Los Angeles, CA 90028
Phone 323-960-2590
Fax   323-960-2591
URL   www.producersguild.com

SCREEN ACTORS GUILD (SAG-LA)
5757 Wilshire Blvd.
Los Angeles, CA 90036-3600
Phone 323-954-1600 (Main Line)
        323-549-6737 (Actors to Locate)
        323-549-6644 (Affirmative Action)
        323-549-6745 (Agent Contracts)
        323-549-6858 (Commercial/
        Music Videos/Infomercials)
        323-549-6654 (Communications)
        323-549-6755 (Dues Information)
        323-549-6811 (Extras/Production
        Services)
        323-549-6850 (Industrial/Educa-
        tional/Interactive/CD-ROM)
        323-549-6627 (Legal Affairs)
        323-549-6778 (Membership
        Services)
        323-549-6769 (New
        Memberships)
        323-549-6835 (TV Contracts)
        323-549-6828 (Theatrical Motion
        Pictures)
        323-549-6505/800-205-7716
        (Residuals)
        323-549-6708 (SAG Foundation)
        323-549-6023 (SAG Jobs Hotline)
        818-954-9400 (SAG Pension &
        Health)
        323-549-6869 (Signatory
        Records)
        323-549-6864 (Singers'
        Representatives)
        323-549-6794 (Station 12)
        323-549-6560 (Stunts/Safety)
Fax   323-549-6648
URL   www.sag.org

SCREEN ACTORS GUILD (SAG-NY)
1515 Broadway, 44th Fl.
New York, NY 10036
Phone 212-944-1030
Fax   212-944-6774
URL   www.sag.org

SOCIETY OF STAGE DIRECTORS & CHOREOGRAPHERS (SSDC)
1501 Broadway, Ste. 1701
New York, NY 10036-5653
Phone 212-391-1070
Fax   212-302-6195
URL   www.ssdc.org

TALENT MANAGERS ASSOCIATION (TMA)
12358 Ventura Blvd., #611
Studio City, CA 91604
Phone 310-205-8495
Fax   818-765-2903
Email info@talentmanagers.org
URL   www.talentmanagers.org

WRITERS GUILD OF AMERICA EAST (WGAE)
555 W. 57th St., Ste. 1230
New York, NY 10019
Phone 212-767-7800
Fax   212-582-1909
URL   www.wgaeast.org

WRITERS GUILD OF AMERICA WEST (WGAW)
7000 W. Third St.
Los Angeles, CA 90048-4329
Phone 323-951-4000
        323-782-4502 (Agency Listing)
Fax   323-782-4800
URL   www.wga.org

LIBRARIES AND MUSEUMS

ACADEMY OF MOTION PICTURE ARTS & SCIENCES—MARGARET HERRICK LIBRARY
333 S. La Cienega Blvd.
Beverly Hills, CA 90211
Phone 310-247-3035 (General
                        Information)
          310-247-3020 (Reference)
Fax   310-657-5193
URL   www.oscars.org

AMERICAN MUSEUM OF MOVING IMAGES
36-01 35th Ave.
Astoria, NY 11106
Phone 718-784-4520
Fax   718-784-4681
URL   www.ammi.org

BEVERLY HILLS PUBLIC LIBRARY
444 N. Rexford Dr.
Beverly Hills, CA 90210
Phone 310-288-2200
          310-288-2244 (Reference)

GOLDWYN HOLLYWOOD BRANCH LIBRARY (LAPL)
(Special entertainment industry collections)
1623 N. Ivar Ave.
Los Angeles, CA 90028
Phone 323-856-8260
Fax   323-467-5707
URL   www.lapl.org

LOS ANGELES PUBLIC LIBRARY
630 W. Fifth St.
Los Angeles, CA 90071
Phone 213-228-7000
Fax   213-228-7229
URL   www.lapl.org

MUSEUM OF TELEVISION & RADIO (LA)
465 N. Beverly Dr.
Beverly Hills, CA 90210
Phone 310-786-1000
Fax   310-786-1086
URL   www.mtr.org

MUSEUM OF TELEVISION & RADIO (NY)
25 W. 52nd St.
New York, NY 10019
Phone 212-621-6600
Fax   212-621-6700
URL   www.mtr.org

NEW YORK PUBLIC LIBRARY FOR THE PERFORMING ARTS AT THE ANNEX— DANCE, THEATRE, MUSIC, RECORDED SOUND ARCHIVE—RESEARCH
521 W. 43rd St.
New York, NY 10036-4396
Phone 212-870-1630
          212-870-1663 (Recordings)
          212-870-1639 (Theater)
          212-870-1657 (Dance)
          212-870-1650 (Music)
URL   www.nypl.org

NEW YORK PUBLIC LIBRARY FOR THE PERFORMING ARTS AT THE MID-MANHATTAN LIBRARY— CIRCULATING DIVISION
455 Fifth Ave., 4th Fl.
New York, NY 10016-0122
Phone 212-870-1630
URL   www.nypl.org

NEW YORK PUBLIC LIBRARY— HUMANITIES AND SOCIAL SCIENCES LIBRARIES
Fifth Ave. & 42nd St.
New York, NY 10018-2788
Phone 212-930-0831
          212-930-0830 (Reference)
URL   www.nypl.org

WRITERS GUILD FOUNDATION—
JAMES R. WEBB MEMORIAL LIBRARY
7000 W. Third St.
Los Angeles, CA 90048-4329
Phone 323-782-4544
Fax   323-782-4695
URL   www.wga.org

LITERARY AGENTS

ARIZONA

CREATIVE AUTHORS AGENCY
12212 Paradise Village Pkwy
South #403-C
Phoenix, AZ 85032
(602) 953-0164

CALIFORNIA

A TOTAL ACTING EXPERIENCE
20501 Ventura Blvd #399
Woodland Hills, CA 91364-2350

ABLAZE ENT. INC.
1040 N. Las Palmas Ave, Bldg 30
Los Angeles, CA 90038
(323) 871-2202

ABOVE THE LINE AGENCY
9200 Sunset Blvd #804
West Hollywood, CA 90069
(310) 859-6115

ACME TALENT & LITERARY AGENCY
6310 San Vicente Blvd #520
Los Angeles, CA 90048
(323) 954-2263

AGENCY FOR THE PERFORMING ARTS
9200 Sunset Blvd #900
Los Angeles, CA 90069
(310) 888-4200

AGENCY, THE
1800 Avenue of the Stars #400
Los Angeles, CA 90067
(310) 551-3000

ALLEN TALENT AGENCY
3832 Wilshire Blvd 2nd Floor
Los Angeles, CA 90010-3221
(213) 896-9372

ALPERN GROUP, THE
15645 Royal Oak Road
Encino, CA 91436
(818) 528-1111

ANGEL CITY TALENT
1680 Vine St #716
Los Angeles, CA 90028
(323) 463-1680

ARTISTS AGENCY, THE
10000 Santa Monica Blvd #305
Los Angeles, CA 90067
(310) 277-7779

ARTISTS GROUP, LTD., THE
10100 Santa Monica Blvd #2490
Los Angeles, CA 90067
(310) 552-1100

BECSEY, WISDOM, KALAJIAN
9200 Sunset Blvd #820
Los Angeles, CA 90069
(310) 550-0535

BENNETT AGENCY, THE
1129 State Street #9
Santa Barbara, CA 93101
(805) 963-7600

BOHRMAN AGENCY, THE
8899 Beverly Blvd. #811
Los Angeles, CA 90048
(310) 550-5444

BRANDT COMPANY, THE
15159 Greenleaf St.
Sherman Oaks, CA 91403
(818) 783-7747

BRODER/KURLAND/WEBB/UFFNER
9242 Beverly Blvd #200
Beverly Hills, CA 90210
(310) 281-3400

BROWN, BRUCE AGENCY
1033 Gayley Ave #207
Los Angeles, CA 90024
(310) 208-1835

BUCHWALD, DON & ASSOCIATES
6500 Wilshire Blvd #2200
Los Angeles, CA 90048
(310) 655-7400

CAREER ARTISTS INTERNATIONAL
11030 Ventura Blvd #3
Studio City, CA 91604
(818) 980-1315

**CATALYST LITERARY &
TALENT AGENCY**
(818) 597-8335

CAVALERI & ASSOCIATES
178 S. Victory Blvd #205
Burbank, CA 91502
(818) 955-9300

CHASIN AGENCY, INC., THE
8899 Beverly Blvd. #716
Los Angeles, CA 90048
(310) 278-7505

CONTEMPORARY ARTISTS, LTD.
610 Santa Monica Blvd #202
Santa Monica, CA 90401
(310) 395-1800

COPPAGE COMPANY, THE
3500 West Olive #1420
Burbank, CA 91505
(818) 953-4163

CORALIE JR. THEATRICAL AGENCY
4789 Vineland Ave #100
North Hollywood, CA 91602
(818) 766-9501

DAVID & DAVID AGENCY
7461 Beverly Blvd #402
Los Angeles, CA 90036
(323) 634-7777

DIVERSE TALENT GROUP, INC.
1875 Century Park East #2250
Los Angeles, CA 90067
(310) 201-6565

DOUROUX & CO.
815 Manhattan Ave. Suite D
Manhattan Beach, CA 90266
(310) 379-3435

DYTMAN & ASSOCIATES
9200 Sunset Blvd #809
Los Angeles, CA 90069
(310) 274-8844

ELLECHANTE TALENT AGENCY
274 Spazier Avenue
Burbank, CA 91502
(818) 557-3025

ENDEAVOR AGENCY, THE
9701 Wilshire Blvd, 10th Floor
Beverly Hills, CA 90212
(310) 248-2000

**EPSTEIN-WYCKOFF-CORSA-ROSS
& ASSOCIATES**
280 South Beverly Dr #400
Beverly Hills, CA 90212
(310) 278-7222

ES AGENCY, THE
110 East D Street #B
Benicia, CA 94510
(707) 748-7394

FAVORED ARTIST AGENCY
8811 Burton Way
Los Angeles, CA 90048
(310) 859-8556

FIELD-CECH-MURPHY AGENCY
12725 Ventura Blvd #D
Studio City, CA 91604
(818) 980-2001

FILM ARTISTS ASSOCIATES
13563 1/2 Ventura Blvd
2nd Floor
Sherman Oaks, CA 91423
(818) 386-9669

FILM-THEATER ACTORS EXCHANGE
390 28th Avenue #3
San Francisco, CA 94121
(415) 379-9308

FREED, BARRY COMPANY, INC., THE
2040 Avenue of the Stars #400
Los Angeles, CA 90067
(310) 277-1260

FRIES, ALICE AGENCY, LTD.
1927 Vista Del Mar Ave
Los Angeles, CA 90068
(323) 464-1404

GAGE GROUP, INC., THE
9255 Sunset Blvd #515
Los Angeles, CA 90069
(310) 859-8777

GARRICK, DALE INTERNATIONAL
8831 Sunset Blvd
Los Angeles, CA 90069
(310) 657-2661

GEDDES AGENCY
8430 Santa Monica Blvd #200
West Hollywood, CA 90069
(323) 848-2700

GELFF, LAYA AGENCY
16133 Ventura Blvd #700
Encino, CA 91436
(818) 996-3100

GERARD, PAUL TALENT AGENCY
11712 Moorpark St #112
Studio City, CA 91604
(818) 769-7015

GERSH AGENCY, INC., THE
232 North Canon Dr #201
Beverly Hills, CA 90210
(310) 274-6611

GORDON, MICHELLE & ASSOCIATES
260 South Beverly Dr #308
Beverly Hills, CA 90212
(310) 246-9930

**GUSAY, CHARLOTTE LITERARY
AGENT/ARTISTS REPRESENTATIVE**
10532 Blythe Ave.
Los Angeles, CA 90064
(310) 559-0831

GROSSMAN, LARRY & ASSOCIATES
211 South Beverly Dr #206
Beverly Hills, CA 90212
(310) 550-8127

HAMILBURG, MITCHELL J. AGENCY
8671 Wilshire Blvd #500
Beverly Hills, CA 90211
(310) 657-1501

HART LITERARY MANAGEMENT
3541 Olive Street
Santa Ynez, CA 93460
(805) 686-7912

HENDERSON/HOGAN AGENCY,INC.
247 South Beverly Dr
Beverly Hills, CA 90212
(310) 274-7815

HERMAN, RICHARD TALENT AGENCY
124 Lasky Dr, 2nd Floor
Beverly Hills, CA 90212
(310) 550-8913

HOHMAN, MAYBANK, LIEB
9229 Sunset Blvd. #700
Los Angeles, CA 90069
(310) 274-4600

HWA TALENT REPRESENTATIVES, INC.
3500 West Olive Ave. #1400
Burbank, CA 91505
(818) 972-4310

INNOVATIVE ARTISTS
1505 Tenth Street
Santa Monica, CA 90401
(310) 656-0400

INTERNATIONAL CREATIVE MGMT
8942 Wilshire Blvd
Beverly Hills, CA 90211
(310) 550-4000

JOHNSON, SUSAN AGENCY, THE
13321 Ventura Blvd #C-1
Sherman Oaks, CA 91423
(818) 986-2205

KALLEN, LESLIE B. AGENCY
15760 Ventura Blvd #700
Encino, CA 91436
(818) 906-2785

**KAPLAN-STAHLER-GUMER
AGENCY, THE**
8383 Wilshire Blvd #923
Beverly Hills, CA 90211
(323) 653-4483

KARG, MICHAEL & ASSOCIATES
1319 Wellesley Ave. #205
Los Angeles, CA 90025
(310) 205-0435

KLANE, JON AGENCY
120 El Camino Dr #112
Beverly Hills, CA 90212
(310) 278-0178

KOHNER, PAUL INC.
9300 Wilshire Blvd #555
Beverly Hills, CA 90212
(310) 550-1060

**KOZLOV, CARY LITERARY
REPRESENTATION**
11911 San Vicente Blvd. #348
Los Angeles, CA 90049
(310) 843-2211

LAKE, CANDACE AGENCY, INC., THE
9200 Sunset Blvd #820
Los Angeles, CA 90069
(310) 247-2115

LARCHMONT LITERARY AGENCY
444 North Larchmont Blvd. #200
Los Angeles, CA 90004
(323) 856-3070

LENHOFF & LENHOFF
9200 Sunset Blvd #830
Los Angeles, CA 90069
(310) 550-3900

LENNY, JACK ASSOCIATES
9454 Wilshire Blvd #600
Beverly Hills, CA 90212
(310) 271-2174

LICHTMAN/SALNERS CO.
12216 Moorpark Street
Studio City, CA 91604
(818) 655-9898

LUKER, JANA TALENT AGENCY
1923 1/2 Westwood Blvd #3
Los Angeles, CA 90025
(310) 441-2822

LYNNE & REILLY AGENCY
10725 Vanowen St
North Hollywood, CA 91605-6402
(323) 850-1984

MAJOR CLIENTS AGENCY
345 North Maple Dr #395
Beverly Hills, CA 90210
(310) 205-5000

MARIS AGENCY
17620 Sherman Way #213
Van Nuys, CA 91406
(818) 708-2493

MARKWOOD COMPANY, THE
1813 Victory Blvd
Glendale, CA 91201
(818) 401-3644

**MEDIA ARTISTS GROUP/
CAPITAL ARTISTS**
6404 Wilshire Blvd #950
Los Angeles, CA 90048
(323) 658-7434

METROPOLITAN TALENT AGENCY
4526 Wilshire Blvd
Los Angeles, CA 90010
(323) 857-4500

MILLER, STUART M. CO., THE
11684 Ventura Blvd #225
Studio City, CA 91604
(818) 506-6067

OMNIPOP, INC.
10700 Ventura Blvd, 2nd Fl
Studio City, CA 91604
(818) 980-9267

ORANGE GROVE GROUP, INC., THE
12178 Ventura Blvd #205
Studio City, CA 91604
(818) 762-7498

ORIGINAL ARTISTS
9465 Wilshire Blvd. #840
Beverly Hills, CA 90212
(310) 277-1251

PANDA TALENT AGENCY
3721 Hoen Ave
Santa Rosa, CA 95405
(707) 576-0711

PARADIGM
10100 Santa Monica Blvd #2500
Los Angeles, CA 90067
(310) 277-4400

PLESHETTE, LYNN LITERARY AGENCY
2700 North Beachwood Dr
Hollywood, CA 90068
(323) 465-0428

PREFERRED ARTISTS
16633 Ventura Blvd #1421
Encino, CA 91436
(818) 990-0305

PREMINGER, JIM AGENCY, THE
450 N. Roxbury Dr.
Penthouse 1050
Beverly Hills, CA 90210
(310) 860-1116

PREMIER ARTISTS AGENCY
400 S. Beverly Dr. #214
Beverly Hills, CA 90212
(310) 284-4064

PRICE, FRED R. LITERARY AGENCY
14044 Ventura Blvd #201
Sherman Oaks, CA 91423
(818) 763-6365

PRIVILEGE TALENT AGENCY
14542 Ventura Blvd. #209
Sherman Oaks, CA 91403
(818) 386-2377

QUILLCO AGENCY
3104 West Cumberland Ct
Westlake Village, CA 91362
(805) 495-8436

RICHLAND AGENCY, THE
2828 Donald Douglas Loop North
Santa Monica, CA 90405
(310) 571-1833

ROBINS, MICHAEL D & ASSOCIATES
23241 Ventura Blvd. #300
Woodland Hills, CA 91364
(818) 343-1755

**ROMANO, CINDY MODELING &
TALENT AGENCY**
1555 S Palm Cyn Dr #D-102
Palm Springs, CA 92264
(760) 323-3333

ROSE, BRANT AGENCY
10537 Santa Monica Blvd #305
Los Angeles, CA 90025
(310) 470-4243

ROTHMAN AGENCY, THE
9465 Wilshire Blvd #840
Beverly Hills, CA 90212
(310) 247-9898

SANFORD-GROSS & ASSOCIATES
1015 Gayley Ave #301
Los Angeles, CA 90024
(310)208-2100

SARNOFF COMPANY, INC., THE
10 Universal City Plaza #2000
Universal City, CA 91608
(818) 754-3708

SCAGNETTI, JACK
5118 Vineland Ave #102
North Hollywood, CA 91601
(818) 762-3871

SHAFER & ASSOCIATES
9000 Sunset Blvd #808
Los Angeles, CA 90069
(310) 888-1240

SHAPIRA, DAVID & ASSOC., INC.
15821 Ventura Blvd #235
Encino, CA 91436
(818) 906-0322

SHAPIRO-LICHTMAN, INC.
8827 Bevelry Blvd
Los Angeles, CA 90048
(310) 859-8877

SHERMAN, KEN & ASSOCIATES
9507 Santa Monica Blvd #212
Beverly Hills, CA 90210
(310) 273-8840

SIEGEL, JEROME S. ASSOCIATES
1680 North Vine St. #617
Hollywood, CA 90028
(323) 466-0185

SINDELL, RICHARD & ASSOCIATES
8271 Melrose Ave #202
Los Angeles, CA 90046
(323) 653-5051

SMITH, GERALD K. & ASSOCIATES
(323) 849-5388

SMITH, SUSAN & ASSOCIATES
121 North San Vicente Blvd
Beverly Hills, CA 90211
(323) 852-4777

**SOLOWAY, GRANT, KOPALOFF
& ASSOCIATES**
6399 Wilshire Blvd #414
Los Angeles, CA 90048
(323) 782-1854

SORICE, CAMILLE TALENT AGENCY
13412 Moorpark St #C
Sherman Oaks, CA 91423
(818) 995-1775

STARLING, CARYN TALENT AGENCY
4728 Greenbush Ave.
Sherman Oaks, CA 91423
(818) 986-8938

STARS, THE AGENCY
23 Grant Avenue, 4th Floor
San Francisco, CA 94108
(415) 421-6272

STARWILL PRODUCTIONS
433 N. Camden Dr., 4th Floor
Beverly Hills, CA 90210
(323) 874-1239

STEIN AGENCY, THE
5125 Oakdale Ave.
Woodland Hills, CA 91364
(818) 594-8990

STONE MANNERS AGENCY, THE
8436 W. 3rd Street #740
Los Angeles, CA 90048
(323) 655-1313

SUMMIT TALENT & LITERARY AGENCY
9454 Wilshire Blvd #320
Beverly Hills, CA 90212
(310) 205-9730

TRIUMPH LITERARY AGENCY
3000 West Olympic Blvd. #1362
Santa Monica, CA 90404
(310) 264-3959

TURTLE AGENCY, THE
7720 B El Camino Real #125
Carlsbad, CA 92009
(760) 632-5857

UNITED ARTISTS TALENT AGENCY
14011 Ventura Blvd. #213
Sherman Oaks, CA 91423
(818) 788-7305

UNITED TALENT AGENCY
9560 Wilshire Blvd, 5th Floor
Beverly Hills, CA 90212
(310) 273-6700

VISION ART MANAGEMENT
9200 Sunset Blvd, Penthouse 1
Los Angeles, CA 90069
(310) 888-3288

WARDEN, WHITE & ASSOCIATES
8444 Wilshire Blvd., 4th Floor
Beverly Hills, CA 90211
(323) 852-1028

WARDLOW & ASSOCIATES
1501 Main Street #204
Venice, CA 90291
(310) 452-1292

WILSON, SHIRLEY & ASSOCIATES
5410 Wilshire Blvd #227
Los Angeles, CA 90036
(323) 857-6977

WORKING ARTISTS TALENT AGENCY
10914 Rathburn Ave
Northridge, CA 91326
(818) 368-8222

WRIGHT, MARION A AGENCY
4317 Bluebell Ave
Studio City, CA 91604
(818) 766-7307

WRITERS & ARTISTS AGENCY (LA)
8383 Wilshire Blvd. #550
Beverly Hills, CA 90211
(323) 866-0900

COLORADO

HODGES, CAROLYN AGENCY
1980 Glenwood Dr
Boulder, CO 80304
(303) 443-4636

MCMAHAN, KELLY AGENCY
5686 S Crocker St #3A
Littleton, CO 80120
(303) 703-3723

WENDLAND, JEFFREY T. AGENCY
265 South 38th St
Boulder, CO 80303
(303) 499-2018

CONNECTICUT

DISCOVERED AGENCY
21 St. James
West Hartford, CT 06107

GARY-PAUL AGENCY, THE
84 Canaan Ct #17
Stratford, CT 06614
(203) 336-0257

TALL TREES DEVELOPMENT GROUP
301 Old Westport Rd
Wilton, CT 06897
(203) 762-5748

WASHINGTON D.C.

**GABALDON, THERESA A.
LITERARY AGENT**
2020 Pennsylvania Ave, NW #222
Washington, DC 20006

SCHECTER, LEONA P. LIT. AGENCY
3748 Huntington St, NW
Washington, DC 20015
(202) 362-9040

FLORIDA

BERG AGENCY, INC.
15908 Eagle River Way
Tampa, FL 33624
(813) 877-5533

CAMERON, MARSHALL AGENCY
19667 NE 20th Lane
Lawtey, FL 32058
(904) 964-7013

COCONUT GROVE TALENT AGENCY
3525 Vista Ct
Coconut Grove, FL 33133
(305) 858-3002

HURT AGENCY, INC.
400 New York Ave, North #207
Winter Park, FL 32789
(407) 740-5700

LEGACIES
501 Woodstork Circle, Perico Bay
Bradenton, FL 34209
(941) 792-9159

MERDON MARKETING, INC.
6941 Selillian Court
Stuart, FL 34997
(561) 287-0616

MIAMI CONSULTING GROUP, INC.
5735 San Vicente St
Coral Gables, FL 33146
(305) 661-4425

REVERIE LITERARY AGENCY
6822 22nd Ave, North #121
Saint Petersburg, FL 33710
(727) 864-2106

SALPETER AGENCY, THE
7461 West Country Club Dr North #406
Sarasota, FL 34243
(941) 359-0568

STAFFORD, GLENDA & ASSOCIATES
14953 Newport Rd #100
Clearwater, FL 33764
(727) 535-1374

TEL-SCREEN INT'L, INC.
2659 Carambola Circle North
Building A #404
Coconut Creek, FL 33066
(954) 974-2251

GEORGIA

CALIFORNIA ARTISTS AGENCY
3053 Centerville Rosebud Rd
Snellville, GA 30039
(770) 982-1477

GENESIS AGENCY, THE
1465 Northside Dr #120
Atlanta, GA 30318
(404) 350-9212

K.T. ENTERPRISES
2605 Ben Hill Rd
East Point, GA 30344
(404) 346-3191

MC BRAYER LITERARY AGENCY
2483 Wawona Dr
Atlanta, GA 30319
(404) 634-1045

MONROE-PRITCHARD-MONROE
722 Ridgecreek Dr
Clarkston, GA 30021
(404) 296-4000

SUNSHINE AGENCY, THE
2687 Mccollum Pkwy. #113
Kennesaw, GA 30144
(770) 795-8175

TALENT SOURCE
107 East Hall St
Savannah, GA 31401
(912) 232-9390

WRITERSTORE
2004 Rockledge Rd, NE
Atlanta, GA 30324
(404) 874-6260

IDAHO

AUTHOR'S AGENCY, THE
3355 North Five Mile Rd #332
Boise, ID 83713-3925
(208) 376-5477

ILLINOIS

AGENCY CHICAGO
601 South La Salle St #600-A
Chicago, IL 60605

BRYAN, MARCUS & ASSOCIATES
2970 Maria Avenue #224
Northbrook, IL 60062
(847) 579-0030

**BULGER, KELVIN C.,
ATTORNEY AT LAW**
11 East Adams #604
Chicago, IL 60603
(312) 692-1002

FOR WRITERS ONLY
220 South State St #1320
Chicago, IL 60604
(773) 769-6350

HAMILTON, SHIRLEY, INC.
333 East Ontario Ave #302B
Chicago, IL 60611
(312) 787-4700

JOHNSON, SUSANNE
TALENT AGENCY, LTD.
108 West Oak St
Chicago, IL 60610
(312) 642-8151

K.P. AGENCY
40 East 9th Street #302
Chicago, IL 60605
(312) 922-8801

ORENTAS, DALIA LITERARY AGENT
6128 North Damen Ave
Chicago, IL 60659
(312) 338-6392

SIEGAN & WEISMAN, LTD.
29 S. La Salle
Chicago, IL 60603
(312) 782-1212

SILVER SCREEN PLACEMENTS INC.
602 65th St
Downers Grove, IL 60516
(708) 963-2124

STEWART TALENT
MANAGEMENT CORP.
58 West Huron
Chicago, IL 60610
(312) 943-3226

WHISKEY HILL ENTERTAINMENT
1000 South Williams St
P O Box 606
Westmont,IL 60559-0606
(630) 852-5023

INDIANA

INTERNATIONAL LEONARDS CORP
3612 North Washington Blvd
Indianapolis, IN 46205

JEZ ENTERPRISES
227 Village Way
South Bend, IN 46619
(219) 233-3059

JOINT VENTURE AGENCY
2927 Westbrook Dr #110B
Fort Wayne, IN 46805
(219) 484-1832

KANSAS

JACKSON ARTISTS CORPORATION
7251 Lowell Drive
Overland Park, KS 66204
(913) 384-6688

MASSACHUSETTS

CREATIVE CAREER MANAGEMENT
84 Spruce Run Dr
Brewster, MA 02631
(508) 896-9351

POWLEY, M.A. LITERARY AGENCY
56 Arrowhead Road
Weston, MA 02193
(781) 899-8386

MICHIGAN

GRACE COMPANY, THE
829 Langdon Ct
Rochester Hills, MI 48307
(248) 868-5994

ALJOUNY, JOSEPH S.
29205 Greening Blvd.
Farmington Hills, MI 48334-2945
(248) 932-0090

MINNESOTA

OTITIS MEDIA
1926 Dupont Ave, South
Minneapolis, MN 55403
(612) 377-4918

NEW JERSEY

BROWN, ELLEN AGENCY
211 Clubhouse Dr
Middletown, NJ 07748
(201) 615-0310

REGENCY LITERARY INT'L AGENCY
285 Verona Ave
Newark, NJ 07104
(201) 485-2692

STARFLIGHT AGENCY, THE
75 Troy Drive #C
Springfield, NJ 07081
(908) 964-9292

NEW YORK

ABRAMS ARTISTS AGENCY
275 Seventh Ave, 26th Fl
New York, NY 10001
(646) 486-4600

ADAMS, BRET LTD.
448 West 44th St
New York, NY 10036
(212) 765-5630

AMATO, MICHAEL AGENCY
1650 Broadway, Suite 307
New York, NY 10019
(212) 247-4456

AGENCY FOR THE PERFORMING ARTS
888 7th Ave
New York, NY 10106
(212) 582-1500

AMRON DEVELOPMENT, INC.
77 Horton Pl
Syosset, NY 11791
(516) 364-0238

AMSTERDAM, MARCIA AGENCY
41 West 82nd St
New York, NY 10024-5613
(212) 873-4945

ARTISTS AGENCY, INC.
230 West 55th Street #29D
New York, NY 10019
(212) 245-6960

BERMAN, BOALS & FLYNN, INC.
208 West 30th Street, #401
New York, NY 10001
(212) 868-1068

LILLIE BLAYZE AGENCY, INC.
3000 Marcus Ave #Ll08
Lake Success, NY 11042

BORCHARDT, GEORGES INC.
136 East 57th St
New York, NY 10022
(212) 753-5785

BROWN, CURTIS, LTD.
10 Astor Pl
New York, NY 10003
(212) 473-5400

BROWNE, PEMA, LTD.
Pine Rd, Hcr Box 104B
Neversink, NY 12765
(914) 985-2936

BUCHWALD, DON & ASSOCIATES
10 East 44th St
New York, NY 10017
(212) 867-1070

CARASSO, JOSEPH MARTIN, ESQ.
305 Broadway #1204
New York, NY 10007
(212) 732-0500

CARRY-WILLIAMS AGENCY
49 West 46 Street
New York, NY 10036
(212) 768-2793

CARVAINIS, MARIA AGENCY
1350 Ave of the Americas #2950
New York, NY 10019
(212) 245-6365

DEE MURA ENTERPRISES, INC.
269 West Shore Dr
Massapequa, NY 11758
(516) 795-1616

DONADIO & ASHWORTH, INC.
121 West 27th St
New York, NY 10001
(212) 691-8077

DUVA-FLACK ASSOCIATES, INC.
200 West 57th Street #1008
New York, NY 10019
(212) 957-6000

EARTH TRACKS ARTISTS AGENCY
4809 Ave, North #286
Brooklyn, NY 11234

**FREEDMAN, ROBERT A.
DRAMATIC AGENCY, INC.**
1501 Broadway #2310
New York, NY 10036
(212) 840-5760

GERSH AGENCY, INC., THE
130 West 42nd St
New York, NY 10036
(212) 997-1818

GURMAN, SUSAN AGENCY, THE
865 West End Ave #15A
New York, NY 10025
(212) 749-4618

HASHAGEN, RICK & ASSOCIATES
157 West 57th St
New York, NY 10019
(212) 315-3130

HOGENSON, BARBARA AGENCY, INC.
165 West End Ave #19-C
New York, NY 10023
(212) 874-8084

HUDSON AGENCY, THE
3 Travis Ln.
Montrose, NY 10548
(914) 737-1475

INTERNATIONAL CREATIVE MGMT
40 West 57th St
New York, NY 10019
(212) 556-5600

JANSON, MARILYN JUNE
Literary Agency
4 Alder Ct
Selden, NY 11784
(516) 696-4661

KALLIOPE ENTERPRISES, INC.
15 Larch Dr
New Hyde, NY 11040
(516) 248-2963

KERIN-GOLDBERG ASSOCIATES, INC.
155 East 55th St
New York, NY 10022
(212) 838-7373

KETAY, JOYCE AGENCY, INC., THE
1501 Broadway #1908
New York, NY 10036
(212) 354-6825

KING, ARCHER, LTD.
244 West 54th St., 12th Fl.
New York, NY 10019
(212) 765-3103

KINGDOM INDUSTRIES LTD.
118-11 195th St
P O Box 310
Saint Albans, NY 11412-0310
(718) 949-9804

KMA AGENCY
11 Broadway, Suite 1101
New York, NY 10004
(212) 581-4610

**KOZAK, OTTO LITERARY &
MOTION PICTURE AGENCY**
114 Coronado Street
Atlantic Beach, NY 11509

LASERSON CREATIVE
358 13th St
Brooklyn, NY 11215
(718) 832-1785

LIONIZE, INC.
2020 Broadway #2A
New York, NY 10023
(212) 579-5414

LITERARY GROUP INT'L, THE
270 Lafayette St #1505
New York, NY 10012
(212) 274-1616

LORD, STERLING LITERISTIC, INC.
65 Bleecker St.
New York, NY 10012
(212) 780-6050

LUEDTKE AGENCY, THE
1674 Broadway, #7A
New York, NY 10019
(212) 765-9564

MARKSON, ELAINE LITERARY AGENCY
44 Greenwich Ave.
New York, NY 10011
(212) 243-8480

MATSON, HAROLD, CO., INC.
276 Fifth Ave.
New York, NY 10001
(212) 679-4490

MC INTOSH AND OTIS, INC.
353 Lexington Ave.
New York, NY 10016
(212) 687-7400

MEYERS, ALLAN S. AGENCY
105 Court St.
Brooklyn, NY 11201

MILESTONE LITERARY AGENCY
247 West 26th St #3A
New York, NY 10001
(212) 691-0560

MORRIS, WILLIAMS AGENCY, INC.
1325 Ave of the Americas
New York, NY 10019
(212) 586-5100

MORRISON, HENRY, INC.
105 South Bedford Rd #306-A
Mount Kisco, NY 10549
(914) 666-3500

OMNIBUS PRODUCTIONS
184 Thompson St #1-G
New York, NY 10012
(212) 995-2941

OMNIPOP, INC. TALENT AGENCY
55 West Old Country Rd
Hicksville, NY 11801
(516) 937-6011

OSCARD, FIFI AGENCY, INC.
24 West 40th St, 17th Floor
New York, NY 10018
(212) 764-1100

PALMER, DOROTHY AGENCY
235 West 56th St. #24K
New York, NY 10019
(212) 765-4280

PARAMUSE ARTISTS ASSOCIATION
25 Central Park West, #1B
New York, NY 10023
(212) 758-5055

PEREGRINE WHITTLESEY AGENCY
345 East 80th Street
New York, NY 10021
(212) 737-0153

PROFESSIONAL ARTISTS UNLTD.
321 West 44th Street #605
New York, NY 10036
(212) 247-8770

RAINES AND RAINES
71 Park Ave
New York, NY 10016
(212) 684-5160

ROBBINS OFFICE, THE
405 Park Avenue, 9th Floor
New York, NY 10022
(212) 223-0720

ROBERTS, FLORA, INC.
157 West 57th St
New York, NY 10019
(212) 355-4165

**SANDERS, VICTORIA
LITERARY AGENCY**
241 Ave of the Americas
New York, NY 10014
(212) 633-8811

**SCHULMAN, SUSAN
LITERARY AGENCY**
454 West 44th St
New York, NY 10036
(212) 713-1633

SCHWARTZ, LAURENS R., ESQ.
5 East 22nd St #15D
New York, NY 10010-5315

SEIGEL, ROBERT L
67-21f 193rd Ln
Fresh Meadows, NY 11365
(718) 454-7044

SELMAN, EDYTHEA GINIS
LITERARY AGENT
14 Washington Pl
New York, NY 10003
(212) 473-1874

STEELE, LYLE & COMPANY, LTD.
511 East 73rd #7
New York, NY 10021
(212) 288-2981

STERN, MIRIAM, ESQ.
303 East 83rd St
New York, NY 10028
(212) 794-1289

SYDRA TECHNIQUES CORPORATION
481 8th Ave #E24
New York, NY 10001
(212) 631-0009

TALENT REPRESENTATIVES, INC.
20 East 53rd St
New York, NY 10022
(212) 752-1835

TARG, ROSLYN LITERARY AGENCY
105 West 13th St
New York, NY 10011
(212) 206-9390

WRIGHT, ANN REPRESENTATIVES
165 West 46th St #1105
New York, NY 10036-2501
(212) 764-6770

WRITERS & ARTISTS AGENCY
19 West 44th St #1000
New York, NY 10036
(212) 391-1112

OHIO

KICK ENTERTAINMENT
1934 East 123rd St
Cleveland, OH 44106
(216) 791-2515

LE MODELN, INC.
7536 Market St #104
Boardman, OH 44512
(330) 758-4417

TANNERY HILL LITERARY AGENCY
6447 Hiram Ave
Ashtabula, OH 44004
(216) 997-1440

OREGON

BIGGAR, LOIS & ASSOCIATES
8885 Southwest O'Mara St
Portland, OR 97223
(503) 639-3686

QCORP LITERARY AGENCY
4195 SW 185th Ave
Aloha, OR 97007
(503) 649-6038

CREATIVE COMMUNICATIONS
6919 SE Holgate Blvd
Portland, OR 97206
(503) 323-4366

PENNSYLVANIA

GOOD WRITERS AGENCY, THE
113 Henry Hudson Dr
Delmont, PA 15626
(724) 468-0237

SISTER MANIA PRODUCTIONS, INC.
916 Penn St
Brackenridge, PA 15014
(724) 226-2964

TOAD HALL, INC.
R.R. 2, Box 2090
Laceyville, PA 18623
(570) 869-2942

WINOKUR AGENCY, THE
5575 North Umberland St
Pittsburgh, PA 15217
(412) 421-9248

WORDSWORTH
230 Cherry Lane Rd
East Stroudsburg, PA 18301
(717) 629-6542

RHODE ISLAND

HANAR COMPANY
34 Fairbanks Ave
Pascoag, RI 02859

REYNOLDS, SUZANNE J. AGENCY
167 Church St
Tiverton, RI 02878

TENNESSEE

CLIENT FIRST AGENCY
2134 Fairfax Ave #A-3
Nashville, TN 37212
(615) 325-4780

HAYES, GIL & ASSOCIATES
5125 Barry Rd
Memphis, TN 38117
(901) 818-0086

MIRAGE ENTERPRISES
5100 Stage Road #4
Memphis, TN 38134
(901) 761-9817

TEXAS

ADLEY, PHILIP AGENCY
157 Tarmarack Dr
May, TX 76857-1649
(915) 784-6849

BEVY CREATIVE ENTERPRISES
7139 Azalea
Dallas, TX 75230
(214) 363-5771

BOYLE, THOMAS D.
2001 Ross Ave #3900
Dallas, TX 75201
(214) 661-8913

BURNAM, CAROLYN AGENCY, THE
4207 Valleyfield St
San Antonio, TX 78222-3714
(210) 337-8268

CREATIVE TALENT AGENCY, INC.
5930 Royal Lane
Dallas, TX 75230
(214) 373-4393

**STANTON & ASSOCIATES
LITERARY AGENCY**
4413 Clemson Dr
Garland TX 75042
(972) 276-5427

TINSLEY, ROBYN L.
2935 Ferndale
Houston, TX 77098

UTAH

OPFAR LITERARY AGENCY
1357 West 800 South
Orem, UT 84058
(801) 224-3836

WALKER TALENT AGENCY, INC.
1080 S. 1500 E #98
Clearfield, UT 84015
(801) 725-2118

VIRGINIA

DEITER LITERARY AGENCY, THE
6207 Fushsimi Court
Burke, VA 22015
(703) 440-8920

FILMWRITERS LITERARY AGENCY
4932 Long Shadow Drive
Midlothian, VA 23112
(804) 744-1718

NIMBUS PRODUCTION GROUP, INC
19999 Ebenezer Church Road
Bluemont, VA 20135
(540) 554-8587

WASHINGTON

CANO AGENCY, THE
8257 Latona Ave, Northeast
Seattle, WA 98115
(206) 522-5974

WISCONSIN

ALLAN, LEE AGENCY
7464 North 107th St
Milwaukee, WI 53224-3706
(414) 357-7708

HAWKINS, A.J. AGENCY
3403 North 92nd St
Milwaukee, Wi 53222
(414) 462-0635

CANADA

KAY, CHARLENE AGENCY
901 Beaudry St #6
Saint Jean/Richelieu, Quebec J3A 1C6
(450) 348-5296

SCREENWRITING RESOURCES ON THE WEB

PROFESSIONAL ASSOCIATIONS

AMERICAN FILM MARKETING ASSOC.
Professional organization and advocate for independent film and television industry. Covers trade and marketing issues, and provides membership info.
http://www.afma.com/

AMERICAN SCREENWRITERS ASSOCIATION
Non-profit screenwriting organization offering networking meetings, seminars, newsletter, screenplay competition, critique service and more.
http://www.asascreenwriters.com/

THE AMERICAN SOCIETY OF JOURNALISTS AND AUTHORS
National organization of independent nonfiction writers.
http://www.asja.org/

CINESTORY
A national nonprofit screenwriting organization based in Chicago. Helps writers find alternative access to the film and television industry.
http://www.cinestory.com/

HORROR WRITERS ASSOCIATION
Horror Writers Association helps promote the interests of writers of horror and dark fantasy.
http://www.horror.org/

MOTION PICTURE ASSOCIATION OF AMERICA
Official site for the MPAA.
http://www.mpaa.org/home.htm

NATION ASSOCIATION OF TELEVISION PROGRAMMING EXECUTIVES (NAPTE)
Official site.
http://www.natpe.org/

ORGANIZATION OF BLACK SCREENWRITERS
This organization was founded to address the lack of African American writers in the entertainment industry, and assists screenwriters in the creation of works for film and television.
http://www.obswriter.com/

THE SCREENWRITER'S WORKSHOP
Non-profit association devoted to the development of new, aspiring screenwriters. Based in the UK.
http://www.lsw.org.uk/

SOCIETY OF CHILDREN'S BOOK WRITERS AND ILLUSTRATORS
Professional organization dedicated to serving the people who write, illustrate, or share an interest in children's literature.
http://www.scbwi.org/

JOB LISTINGS

DONE DEAL
Provides recent and past script and pitch sales in Hollywood, agency lists, screenwriting fundamentals, software reviews and more. Updated daily.
http://www.scriptsales.com/

ENTERTAINMENT JOBS & INTERNSHIPS FOR FILM, TV, CABLE & RADIO

Subscription-based service provides national job listings in the entertainment industry.
http://www.eej.com/featuredjobs/ jobinfo.html

HOLLYWOOD CREATIVE DIRECTORY

One of the most comprehensive job listing boards of legitimate employment positions available in the entertainment industry. The only unpaid postings are in the following categories: Interns, Film Crews—Unpaid and Talent—Unpaid.
http://www.hcdonline.com/jobs/

INK SPOT

Ink Spot Writers' classifieds. Find jobs, contests, chats and events of interest to writers for writers.
http://www.inkspot.com/classifieds

NICKELODEON PRODUCTIONS FELLOWSHIP PROGRAM

The number one rated kids network seeks talented writers for their live action and animated television divisions. Check out the site for additional information and deadlines.
http://www.fellowshipprogram.nick.com

SCREENWRITERS UTOPIA, THE

Resource for aspiring writers has discussion groups, writing tips, a Hollywood Internet directory and interviews with people in the industry.
http://www.screenwritersutopia.com/

SURFVIEW ENTERTAINMENT

This site includes a list of production companies seeking material for development.
http://www.surfview.com/seindlst.htm

COPYRIGHTS & CLEARANCE

COPYRIGHT CLEARANCE CENTER

Online site for the largest licenser of copyright rights for books, websites, articles and more.
http://www.copyright.com/

THE COPYRIGHT WEBSITE

Real world, practical copyright information. Download applications.
http://www.benedict.com/

MOTION PICTURE LICENSING CORP.

Independent copyright licensing service used by studios and independent producers to license their properties.
http://www.mplc.com/index2.htm

NATIONAL CREATIVE REGISTRY

Provides registration services in minutes to screenwriters, songwriters and inventors. Offers registration verification and storage facilities.
http://www.ncronline.com/

U.S. COPYRIGHT OFFICE

Official site of the Library of Congress. Find forms for copyright registration. The best way to protect ownership of your script.
http://lcweb.loc.gov/copyright

WRITERS GUILD INTELLECTUAL PROPERTY REGISTRATION

WGA registration service available to members and non-members alike.
http://www.wga.org/manuals/ registration.html

GUILDS AND UNIONS

AFRICAN AMERICAN ONLINE WRITERS GUILD
Online community for African American writers.
http://www.blackwriters.org

DIRECTORS GUILD OF AMERICA
Articles from the guild's magazine include interviews, reviews and industry updates. With joining information and a history of the Directors Guild.
http://www.dga.org/

HEARTLAND WRITERS GUILD
Not-for-profit organization devoted to helping its members market their writing.
http://www.heartlandwriters.org/

NATIONAL WRITERS UNION
Trade union for freelance writers publishing or working in U.S. markets.
http://www.nwu.org/

THE SCREENWRITERS GUILD
Association founded to guide and educate screenwriters on proven strategies and methodologies.
http://www.screenwritersguild.com/

WRITERS GUILD OF AMERICA
The official site for the Writers Guild of America. A thorough website on Guild information and services for guild members and promising new writers.
http://www.wga.org/

WRITERS GUILD OF AMERICA, EAST
A labor union representing writers—located in the eastern part of America—of motion pictures and television programs, plus online script registration.
http://www.wgaeast.org/

WRITERS GUILD OF CANADA
Represents freelance writers working in film, television, radio and new media production in Canada.
http://www.writersguildofcanada.com/

WRITERS GUILD OF GREAT BRITAIN
Official site of Great Britain's Writers Guild.
http://www.wggb.demon.co.uk/

INTERVIEW SITES

FADE IN MAGAZINE
Film magazine for screenwriters offers interviews and articles covering all aspects of living and working in Hollywood. Includes subscription forms.
http://www.fadeinmag.com/

HOLLYWOOD SCRIPTWRITER
Trade newspaper focused primarily on screenwriting.
http://www.hollywoodscriptwriter.com/

HOLLYWOODNETWORK.COM
Articles with top screenwriters.
http://www.hollywoodnetwork.com/hn/writing

SCREEN TALK—THE JOURNAL OF INTERNATIONAL SCREENWRITING
Online magazine for writers offering script software, submissions, archived scripts and top stories.
http://www.screentalk.org/

SCRIPT ONLINE COMMUNITY
Essential site for screenwriters applying to various contests and festivals, and those interested in reading interviews with acclaimed Hollywood writers. Online courses are offered through the magazine's classes page.
http://www.scriptmag.com/

LEGAL EXPERTISE

INTERNATIONAL ENTERTAINMENT, MULTIMEDIA & INTELLECTUAL PROPERTY LAW AND BUSINESS NETWORK

Designed as a central reference point for entertainment, multimedia, intellectual property and online professionals, with international links to professional, legal and business services. It also offers a new, downloadable contract of the month.
http://www.medialawyer.com/

MARK LITWACK, ENTERTAINMENT AND MULTIMEDIA ATTORNEY

Mark Litwack's site provides information about how to make film, television and multimedia deals, and how to take care of yourself legally after you sign the contract.
http://www.marklitwak.com/

MULTIMEDIA & ENTERTAINMENT LAW ONLINE NEWS

Very comprehensive site dealing with all areas of entertainment law.
http://www.ibslaw.com/melon

PAUL D. SUPNIK LAW OFFICES

Offers a full search engine of entertainment law links and resources, from downloadable contracts to dispute resolution.
http://www.supnik.com/

THE PUBLISHING LAW CENTER

Articles on legal issues of concern to writers, covering contracts, fair use, public domain, etc.
http://www.publaw.com/

LITERARY AGENTS

AUTHORASSIST

Provides assistance with landing an editor or literary agent in the competitive world of publishing. Offers customized, personal advice.
http://www.authorassist.com/

HCD'S AGENTS & MANAGERS

The most complete directory of literary agencies and personal management companies.
http://www.hcdonline.com/

LITERARY AGENT

Searchable database of literary book agents.
http://nt9.nyic.com/literaryagent/sch-page.html

MOVIE BYTES

Comprehensive searchable database of literary agents.
http://www.moviebytes.com/agencies.cfm

SCREENWRITERS 101

Offers online advice for new screenwriters looking for the appropriate literary agents.
http://www.screenwriters101.com/

WRITER'S GUIDE TO LITERARY AGENTS

Annual publication offers the amateur writer information that includes who agents are, what they want and how to find them. Read reviews or order.
http://www.emergencepub.com/write21.htm

WRITERS GUILD OF AMERICA

The official site for the Writers Guild of America. A thorough website on Guild information and services for guild members and promising new writers.
http://www.wga.org/

THE WRITER'S WEBSITE: LITERARY AGENTS

Extensive list of literary agencies with contact information.
http://www.writerswebsite.com/links/ Literary_Agents/

SCREENWRITING NEWS

AIN'T IT COOL NEWS

A cinephile from Austin operates this site choc-a-bloc with hot news on upcoming films. Reviews, forums and television info too. No celebrity gossip.
http://www.aint-it-cool-news.com/

CREATIVE SCREENWRITING MAGAZINE

Interviews and information for aspiring and established screenwriters.
http://www.creativescreenwriting.com/

DARK HORIZONS

The latest news and buzz on film projects. Has a Sci-Fi focus but covers everything.
http://www.darkhorizons.com/

DONE DEAL

The latest Hollywood script sales. Updated daily.
http://www.scriptsales.com/ DDScriptSales.htm

ENTERTAINMENT NEWS DAILY

Provides daily entertainment news and press releases from the leading publications.
http://www.entertainmentnewsdaily.com/

FADE IN MAGAZINE

Film magazine for screenwriter's offers interviews and articles covering all aspects of living and working in Hollywood. Includes subscription forms.
http://www.fadeinmag.com/

FILM THREAT

Independent movie magazine offers reviews, interviews, updates on worldwide film festivals and box-office stats.
http://www.filmthreat.com/

THE HOLLYWOOD REPORTER

Online version of the industry trade paper has news of the latest deals covering film, television and music. Also box-office reports, other departments.
http://www.hollywoodreporter.com/

HOLLYWOOD SCRIPTWRITER

Trade newspaper focused primarily on screenwriting.
http://www.hollywoodscriptwriter.com/

INSIDE

Get the inside scoop on the latest events in the world of television, film, music, media and books.
http://www.inside.com/

SCENARIO: THE MAGAZINE OF SCREENWRITING ART

Quarterly publication offering independent and classic screenplays, interviews, articles, events and other screenwriting-related news
http://www.scenariomag.com/subscribe/ info.html

VARIETY.COM

Features film industry articles and breaking news, festival information, film reviews, an event calendar and magazine subscription details.
http://www.variety.com/

WRITERS GUILD OF AMERICA—NEWS

Latest news and information from the WGA.
http://www.wga.org/pr

ONLINE SEMINARS

ABSOLUTE WRITE
A web site dedicated to cover all writing mediums including screenplay and play-writing. The screenplay page is comprised of interviews with screenwriters, message boards, live chat rooms to confer with other writers and sample contracts.
http://www.absolutewrite.com/

ALPHA SCRIPTS
An online teaching guide to leading principles of the screenplay. Character traits, character creation, scenes, locations and events are explored.
http://rivalquest.com/alphascripts

CHESTERFIELD FILM COMPANY
Co-sponsored by Paramount Pictures, The Chesterfield Writer's Film Project offers five $20,000 fellowships a year to writers interested in a professional screenwriting career.
http://www.chesterfield-co.com/

CREATE YOUR SCREENPLAY WITH BARRY PEARSON
Screenplay development, beginning the process of writing and other valuable tips are presented on this site. Upcoming seminars lectured by the accomplished writer are listed.
http://www.createyourscreenplay.com/

E-SCRIPT COURSES AND WORKSHOPS FOR SCREEN AND TV WRITERS
Five and ten week classes are offered on television and film screenplays for beginning and advanced artists.
http://www.singlelane.com/escript/escreen.htm

HOLLYWOOD LIT SALES
Free online screenwriting seminar hosted by industry professionals.
http://www.hollywoodlitsales.com/onlineclasses.html

JOHN TRUBY'S WRITER'S STUDIO
Resource guide for scriptwriters provides writing tips and interviews, software guide and information on screenwriters workshops and classes.
http://www.truby.com/

SCREEN TALK—THE JOURNAL OF INTERNATIONAL SCREENWRITING
An online magazine for writers offering script software, submissions, archived scripts and top stories.
http://www.screentalk.org/

SCREENWRITING HELP
An accomplished Hollywood writer evaluates covering story elements and format for the aspiring screenwriter. Articles pertaining to legal, business and marketing aspects to a screenplay are provided.
http://www.concentric.net/~pcbc

SCRIPT ONLINE COMMUNITY
An essential site for screenwriters applying to various contests and festivals, and those interested in reading interviews with acclaimed Hollywood writers. Online courses are offered through the magazine's classes page.
http://www.scriptmag.com/

STUDIO STORY ANALYSIS
No-nonsense site offers tips, and for a fee, story analysis services for screenwriters to help them sell scripts to the studios.
http://home.earthlink.net/~billkros

STEPHAN J. CANNELL ONLINE WRITING SEMINAR

A downloadable lecture, writing exercises, a live three-hour transcript by a top screenwriter are available for purchase. Also included in the seminar are pilots from long-running television series.
http://www.writerswrite.com/seminar

WRITERS GUILD OF AMERICA— MENTOR SERVICE

Online mentor service connecting professional writers with those who aspire to be.
http://www.wga.org/mentors

THE WRITERS STORE

Essential site for writers. Find script writing sofware, story software, Final Draft, Movie Magic Screenwriter and Dramatica Pro. Also seminars, books and resources for feature and television writers.
http://writerscomputer.com

WRITING CLASSES

Fee-based online writing classes.
http://www.writingclasses.com/

WRITINGSCHOOL.COM

Learn fundamentals of screenwriting and understand what makes a successful screenplay work by dissecting its story and characters in a distance education course. Instructed by credited screenwriters from Little Men and Star Quest.
http://www.writingschool.com/ scren201.htm

WRITING FOR FILM

Notes from the pros, software tools and frequently asked questions provide the writer with essential tips to get started on their first draft.
http://www.communicator.com/ writfilm.html

RESEARCH LIBRARIES, SITES & SERVICES

ALL-MOVIE GUIDE

Colossal searchable movie database, with film suggestions, a "plot-finder," interviews, glossary and more. Affiliated with the All-Music Guide.
http://www.allmovie.com/

BARTLETT'S BOOK OF FAMILIAR QUOTATIONS

Over 11,000 literary and historical quotations from Socrates to present day.
http://www.bartleby.com/100

BRAUN RESEARCH LIBRARY

The Southwest Museum in Los Angeles— find information about Native American and early American Western culture.
http://www.southwestmuseum.org/ braun.htm

CHICAGO PUBLIC LIBRARY

Official site for the Chicago Public Library.
http://www.chipublib.org/

ELECTRONIC LIBRARY

Conduct real research over the Internet and find articles on almost any subject under the sun.
http://www.elibrary.com/

ENCYLOPEDIA.COM

Columbia Electronic Encyclopedia—free useful information on almost any topic.
http://www.encyclopedia.com/home.html

FINDERS RESEARCH SERVICES

Find film footage, print media and audio for any subject.
http://www.maxfilmpro.com/advisor/ fi/FindersRes_1

INTERNET MOVIE DATABASE
Award winning site with daily news, articles and an extensive movie credit database featuring more than 180,000 movies. An essential site for the movie lover. Translated into three languages.
http://us.imdb.com/

INTERNET SEARCH FAQ
How to find information, people, research data and almost anything else on the Internet.
http://www.purefiction.com/pages/res1.htm

LEAVEY FOUNDATION FOR HISTORIC PRESERVATION
Over 350 pages of information about American History during the 19th Century. Find information on Victorian clothing, weapons, props and set dressing and reeinactors.
http://main.1ie.com/azra-hist/AZRAHOME.HTM

LIBRARY OF CONGRESS
Conduct real research over the Internet; find articles on any subject.
http://www.loc.gov/

THE MARGARET HERRICK LIBRARY
Research library of the Academy of Motion Picture Arts and Sciences.
http://www.oscars.org/cmps/mhl

MERRIAM WEBSTER DICTIONARY
Online dictionary and thesaurus.
http://www.m-w.com/netdict.htm

THE MUSEUM OF TELEVISION AND RADIO
Presented by the Film Society and home to the Lincoln Center exhibit of the industrys hottest new filmmakers, this site offers the best in electronic masterpieces and aesthetic excellence in films.
http://www.mtr.org/

NASA
Official site. Find information on U.S. space program, aeronautics, earth science and space research.
http://www.nasa.gov/NASA_homepage.html

NEW YORK CITY PUBLIC LIBRARY
Official site for NYC Public Library.
http://www.nypl.org/

THE OLD FARMERS ALMANAC
Information on weather prediction, sunrise tables, planting charts, home remedies and gardening.
http://www.almanac.com/

STATISTICAL ABSTRACT OF THE U.S.
U.S. Census Bureau offers info from reports and records of government and private agencies. Information accessed using Adobe Acrobat.
http://www.census.gov/prod/2/gen/96statab/96statab.html

SCRIPT LIBRARIES

DREW'S SCRIPTS-O-RAMA
Claims to be the most comprehensive index of movie and television scripts on the Internet. Find more than 600 screenplays, transcripts and television scripts.
http://www.script-o-rama.com/

MOVIE PAGE
Online magazine with features, clips, trailers and a long list of movie scripts to choose from.
http://www.movie-page.com/

MOVIE SCRIPTS ONLINE
Large library of Hollywood scripts online. Easy to navigate.
http://www.onlinescripts.cjb.net/

MOVIE WORLD
Hundreds of film and television scripts and transcripts.
http://www.geocities.com/Hollywood/Studio/9910

REEL USA
This site has hundreds of online movie scripts to download.
http://www.reelusa.com/scripts.html

ROSEBUD ELECTRONIC PUBLISHER'S SCRIPTS ON THE NET
Vast database of film scripts. View online or download.
http://www.rosebud.com.br/scripts.htm

SCRIPT SHACK
Find scripts online with this comprehensive movie script database.
http://www.scriptshack.com/

SIMPLY SCRIPTS
Check out this searchable index of scripts and screenplays for television, radio, movies and anime.
http://simplyscripts.com/

SELLING & PITCHING

CINEMA NOW
A forum for watching, making, buying and winning films. An affiliate of Trimark Pictures
http://www.cinemanow.com/

THE CINESTORE
The Cinestore sells film and television scripts, books, audio tapes, and second-hand cameras
http://www.thecinestore.com/

DONE DEAL
Provides recent and past script and pitch sales in Hollywood, agency lists, screenwriting fundamentals, software reviews and more. Updated daily.
http://www.scriptsales.com/

GOOD STORY
Post your script online with logline, synopsis and contact info. Fee based service. An affiliate of Creative Planet.
http://www.goodstory.com/

HOLLYWOOD LIT SALES
Offers writers a forum for writers to sell their material to Hollywood industry professionals. One of the few sites with actual ties to the entertainment industry. Daily spec sales and spec script database. Fee based service.
http://www.hollywoodlitsales.com/

MOVIEBYTES
This site contains tons of information on screenwriting contests and competitions online, with contact information, deadlines and Internet links where available.
http://www.moviebytes.com/

SCRIPTSHARK
IFILMpro's professional script coverage service run by former Hollywood development executives. If a script receives favorable coverage, ScriptShark will work with the writer and introduce them to Hollywood agents and producers. Read writer success stories and find essential tips and advice. Fee based.
http://www.scriptshark.com/

WWW LINK OF ONLINE SCRIPT PITCHES
Offers the title and type of scripts available at the other sites.
http://members.tripod.com/~makulaff

ZOETROPE SCREENPLAYS
American Zoetrope accepts submissions of feature-length screenplays over the Internet for work shopping, feedback, and possible industry contacts.
http://screenplays.fcoppola.com/

SERVICES & ADVICE

COMEDY SCREENPLAYS
Offers a range of contemporary comedy scripts for literary agents and producers looking for something innovative.
http://www.geocities.com/Hollywood/ Hills/3205

CREATIVE SCRIPT SERVICES
Script management service provides networking guidance, agent referrals and marketing strategies for writers for a fee of $300.00 per script.
http://www.thescript.com/

E-SCRIPT SCRIPTWRITING WORKSHOP
Offers five and ten week screenwriting courses and workshops. Includes a message board, enrollment procedures and staff bios.
http://www.singlelane.com/escript

FROM SCRIPT TO SCREEN.COM
Advice about writing television or movie screenplays. Features a free newsletter, industry briefings, assistance for documentaries and news.
http://www.fromscripttoscreen.com/

GLENN SOBEL MANAGEMENT
Agent and personal manager provides screenwriters with access to producers, directors and stars looking to purchase scripts.
http://members.aol.com/WriterMngr

HOW TO GET AN AGENT
Reference guide explores the ins and outs of finding an agent for screenwriters. Includes the WGA list of franchised agents.
http://www.wga.org/agentinfo.html

THE INSIDERS SYSTEM FOR WRITERS
Provides screenplay analysis and networking services to screenwriters. Offers a quarterly entitled Writers Showcase featuring success stories.
http://www.insiderssystem.com/

INTENSIVE SCREENPLAY ANALYSIS
Literary and screenplay consultants provide analysis and script troubleshooting for writers, producers and studio executives.
http://www.scriptzone.com/

INZIDE.COM
Writer advice, info and access to industry insiders.
http://inzide.com/home.cfm

JOHN TRUBY'S WRITER'S STUDIO
Resource guide for scriptwriters provides writing tips and interviews, a software guide, and information on screenwriters workshops and classes.
http://www.truby.com/

LEFT COAST EDITORIAL SERVICES
Resource guide for scriptwriters features script analysis tips, and links to agents and copyright services. Offers fee-based consultations.
http://members.aol.com/coastedit/ Lcintro.htm

THE MASKED MAN

Script consultant offers an overview of his services and provides tips to writers in script analysis and problem solving.
http://www.atelierpix.com/maskedman

MOVIE PITCH

Provides registered members with idea proposal services to Hollywood producers. Offers a CD-ROM which tutors the art of idea development.
http://www.moviepitch.com/questions.htm

MUSE ON FIRE

Script consultant Alex Epstein provides screenplay analysis and makes rewrite suggestions and comments. Includes a release form.
http://modigliani.brandx.net/user/ musofire/screenplay.html

NATIONAL CREATIVE REGISTRY

Provides registration services in minutes to screenwriters, songwriters, and inventors. Offers registration verification and storage facilities.
http://www.ncronline.com/

NINE-ACT STRUCTURE

The secrets of the nine-act structure are revealed at this interesting site. If you're having trouble structuring your script, pay a visit.
http://www.dsiegel.com/film/ Film_home.html

SCREENWRITERS 101

Offers online advice for new screenwriters about how to find the appropriate literary agents.
http://www.screenwriters101.com/

SCREENWRITING HELP

An accomplished Hollywood writer evaluates covering story elements and format for the aspiring screenwriter. Articles pertaining to legal, business and marketing aspects to a screenplay are provided.
http://www.concentric.net/~pcbc

SCRIPTSHARK

Founded by Hollywood professionals, provides online coverage and access to industry insiders.
http://www.scriptshark.com/

STORYBAY.COM

Provides professional coverage and screenwriting advice.
http://storybay.com/

A STORY IS A PROMISE

Site reviews movies to explore principles of storytelling, providing essays on the craft of writing, and hyping the author's book and services.
http://www.storyispromise.com/

STUDIO STORY ANALYSIS

No-nonsense site offers tips, and for a fee, story analysis services for screenwriters to help them sell scripts to the studios.
http://home.earthlink.net/~billkros

WRITERS GUILD OF AMERICA— MENTOR SERVICE

Online mentor service connecting professional writers with those who aspire to be.
http://www.wga.org/mentors

WORDPLAY

Professional secrets for screenplays. Working screenwriter Terry Rosio gives away hints and tips for succeeding in the Hollywood game.
http://www.wordplayer.com/

SOFTWARE & BOOKS

ABRUPT EDGE
Links to available writing guides and resources.
http://www.abruptedge.com/writing.html

CREATIVE SCREENWRITING
Online home of *Creative Screenwriting* magazine, with a section for ordering screenwriting software.
http://www.creativescreenwriting.com/ writeware.html

FINAL DRAFT, INC.
Final Draft—a leader in screenwriting software. Order updates, add-ons and the software online.
http://www.finaldraft.com/

HOLLYWOOD CREATIVE DIRECTORY
IFILM's *Hollywood Creative Directory* contains detailed contact and credit info for producers, distributors, agents & managers, film buyers and more. Available in print or online for subscribers. Also find the HCD Store, with film industry mailing labels and books on acting, directing, screenwriting, producing and filmmaking.
http://www.hcdonline.com/

HOLLYWOOD SCREENPLAY
Site for ordering and finding information about screenplay (and novel writing) software.
http://www.ballisticware.com/

NOVATION
An excellent writer's resource site that has links for ordering screenwriting software.
http://www.novalearn.com/

PAGE 2 STAGE
Word processor designed for playwrights and screenwriters. Features include extensive editing capabilities and Asian-language fonts.
http://www.page2stage.com/

SAMUEL FRENCH BOOKSTORE
Resource for purchasing full length plays and scripts.
http://www.samuelfrench.com/

SCREENPLAY SYSTEMS
The online home of Screenplay Systems Software, makers of Dramatica and the Movie Magic series. Order products online.
http://www.screenplay.com/

SCREENSTYLE.COM
Writers interested in writing for Hollywood will find a catalog of software, books, magazines and audio tapes. Read articles about screenwriting.
http://www.screenstyle.com/

SCREENWRIGHT TUTORIAL
Screenwright, The Craft of Screenwriting is a tutorial that teaches the art of writing a marketable screenplay. Includes purchasing details.
http://www.teleport.com/~cdeemer/book

SCREENWRITING SOFTWARE
Product reviews of all the major screenwriting software programs plus some shareware word processor enhancements.
http://www.communicator.com/ swsoftin.html

SCRIPTWARE
Find information about Scriptware. Order the software online.
http://www.scriptthing.com/

SHOWBIZBOOKS.COM

A huge online directory of books on writing, with links for ordering them.
http://www.showbizbooks.com/ sbproduction.htm

SOPHOCLES SCREENWRITING SOFTWARE

Download a trial version of this story-centered screenwriter's program, then register to keep the software. See screenshots and a features list.
http://www.sophocles.net/

THE WRITER'S RESOURCE HANDBOOK

Online home of The Writer's Resource Handbook.
http://www.allworth.com/Catalog/ WR087C.htm

THE WRITERS STORE

Online store for script writing software, books and any other essential supplies for the screenwriter.
http://writersstore.com/

THE WRITERS STORE—AUDIO BOOKS

Creative-writing bookstore offers audiobooks on the creative process, fiction, drama, screenplays, freelance writing and related topics.
http://writersstore.com/audio_books.htm

SPEC SCRIPT SITES

AMERICAN ZOETROPE

Handsome site for the San Francisco production company founded by Francis Coppola. News, discussion, facilities (including screening room) and screenplay submission details.
http://www.zoetrope.com/

THE BIG DEAL

The Big Deal details a journey through some of screenwriting's most lucrative paydays on various spec scripts.
http://www.bigdealnews.com/

DONE DEAL

Provides recent and past script and pitch sales in Hollywood, agency lists, screenwriting fundamentals, software reviews, and more. Updated daily.
http://www.scriptsales.com/

HOLLYWOOD LIT SALES

Offers writers a forum for writers to sell their material to Hollywood industry professionals. One of the few sites with actual ties to the entertainment industry. Daily spec sales and spec script database. Fee based service.
http://www.hollywoodlitsales.com/

THE SPEC SCRIPT LIBRARY

Source for locating new and original scripts for film and television.
http://www.thesource.com.au/scripts

SCRIPTSHARK

IFILMpro's professional script coverage service run by former Hollywood development executives. If a script receives favorable coverage, ScriptShark will work with writer and introduce them to Hollywood agents and producers. Read writer success stories and find essential tips and advice. Fee based.
http://www.scriptshark.com/

INDICES

ALPHABETICAL INDEX OF CONTESTS

INDEX OF CONTESTS BY GENRE

If not listed here, all genres are accepted.

ACTION/ADVENTURE
Breckenridge Festival of Film
    Screenplay Competion
Fade In: Screenwriting Awards
Filmcontest.com
The 34th Annual Worldfest-Houston
    International Film Festival

ANIMATION
Series Search Writing Contest

BIOGRAPHICAL/HISTORICAL
The 34th Annual Worldfest-Houston
    International Film Festival

BUDGET
Empire Screenplay Contest
Hollywood Screenplay Consultants
    Screenwriting Competition
New Century Writer Awards

CHILDREN/FAMILY
Breckenridge Festival of Film
    Screenplay Competion
The 34th Annual Worldfest-Houston
    International Film Festival

COMEDY
American Accolades Screenwriting
    Competition
Breckenridge Festival of Film
    Screenplay Competion
Fade In: Screenwriting Awards
Filmcontest.com
The 34th Annual Worldfest-Houston
    International Film Festival

DRAMA
American Accolades Screenwriting
    Competition
Breckenridge Festival of Film
    Screenplay Competion
Fade In: Screenwriting Awards
Filmcontest.com
The 34th Annual Worldfest-Houston
    International Film Festival

ETHNIC/MINORITY
Cape Foundation New Writer Award
Cynosure Screenwriting Awards
Film Fleadh Screenplay Competition
New York International Latino Film
    Festival
Walt Disney Studios/ABC Writers
    Fellowship

FEMALE PROTAGONIST
Cynosure Screenwriting Awards

FEMALE WRITER
All She Wrote Screenplay Contest
Moondance Film Festival Contests

FILM NOIR
Fade In: Screenwriting Awards

GAY/LESBIAN
One In Ten Screenplay Competition

LOCATION REQUIREMENTS
Film In Arizona Screenwriting
    Competition
Hong Kong to Hollywood
    Screenplay Contest
Illinois/Chicago Screenwriting
    Competition

Nevada Film Office Annual
  Screenplay Competition
Ohio Independent Screenplay
  Awards
Orange Screenwriting Prize
Set In Philadelphia Screenwriting
  Competition
Set In Texas Screenwriting
  Competition
The Washington State Screenplay
  Competition
Westchester County Film Festival

RESIDENCY
Illinois/Chicago Screenwriting
  Competition
Morrow Screenwriting Fellowship
Ohio Independent Screenplay
  Awards
Orange Screenwriting Prize
Oscar Moore Prize
Samuel Goldwyn Writing Awards
Sir Peter Ustinov Television
  Scriptwriting Award
Society for Cinema Studies Student
  Writing Award
Westchester County Film Festival

ROMANCE
Share the Dream Romantic
  Scriptwriting Contest

SHORT SUBJECT
Bad Kitty Films Screenwriting
  Competition
Daily Script's Get A Life
  Screenwriting Competition
Deer Creek Productions Screenplay
  Competition
Fade In: Screenwriting Awards
Hollywood's Synopsis Writing
  Contest
Kay Snow Writing Awards

Moondance Film Festival Contests
Morrow Screenwriting Fellowship
Project Greenlight
Scriptic Greenlight International
  Scriptwriting Competition
Sir Peter Ustinov Television
  Scriptwriting Award
Troika Magazine Story-to-Film
  Competition
Unique Television Script Writing
  Contest
Warner Bros. Comedy Writers
  Workshop
The 8th Annual Writers Network
  Screenplay & Fiction Contest
Writesafe Present-a-Thon

SCIENCE/SCI-FI
American Accolades Screenwriting
  Competition
The 34th Annual Worldfest-Houston
  International Film Festival

TELEVISION
American Accolades Screenwriting
  Competition
Klasky Csupo Scriptwriting Awards
Monterey County Film Comission
  Screenwriting Competition
The People's Pilot
Scriptapalooza, Inc.and
  Screenplay.com's Screenwriting
  Competition
Scriptwriters Network, Carl Sutter
  Memorial Scriptwriting
  Competition
Sir Peter Ustinov Television
  Scriptwriting Award
Society for Cinema Studies Student
  Writing Award
Square Magazine Screenwriting
  Award

Unique Television Script Writing Contest
Warner Bros. Comedy Writers Workshop
The 8th Annual Writers Network
    Screenplay & Fiction Contest
Writesafe Present-a-Thon

THRILLER/HORROR
American Accolades Screenwriting
    Competition
Fade In: Screenwriting Competition
Oscar Moore Prize
The 34th Annual Worldfest-Houston
    International Film Festival

WEST
Best In West
Film In Arizona Screenwriting
    Competition

YOUNG WRITERS
America's Best High School Writing
    Competition
Kay Snow Writing Awards
Screen Teens
Society for Cinema Studies Student
    Writing Award
UCLA Extension/Diane Thomas
    Screenwriting Awards
The 34th Annual Worldfest-Houston
    International Film Festival

More Screenwriting Books
from IFILMPublishing

To order, call 323.308.3490 or
visit www.hcdonline.com